Gardens of Marrakesh

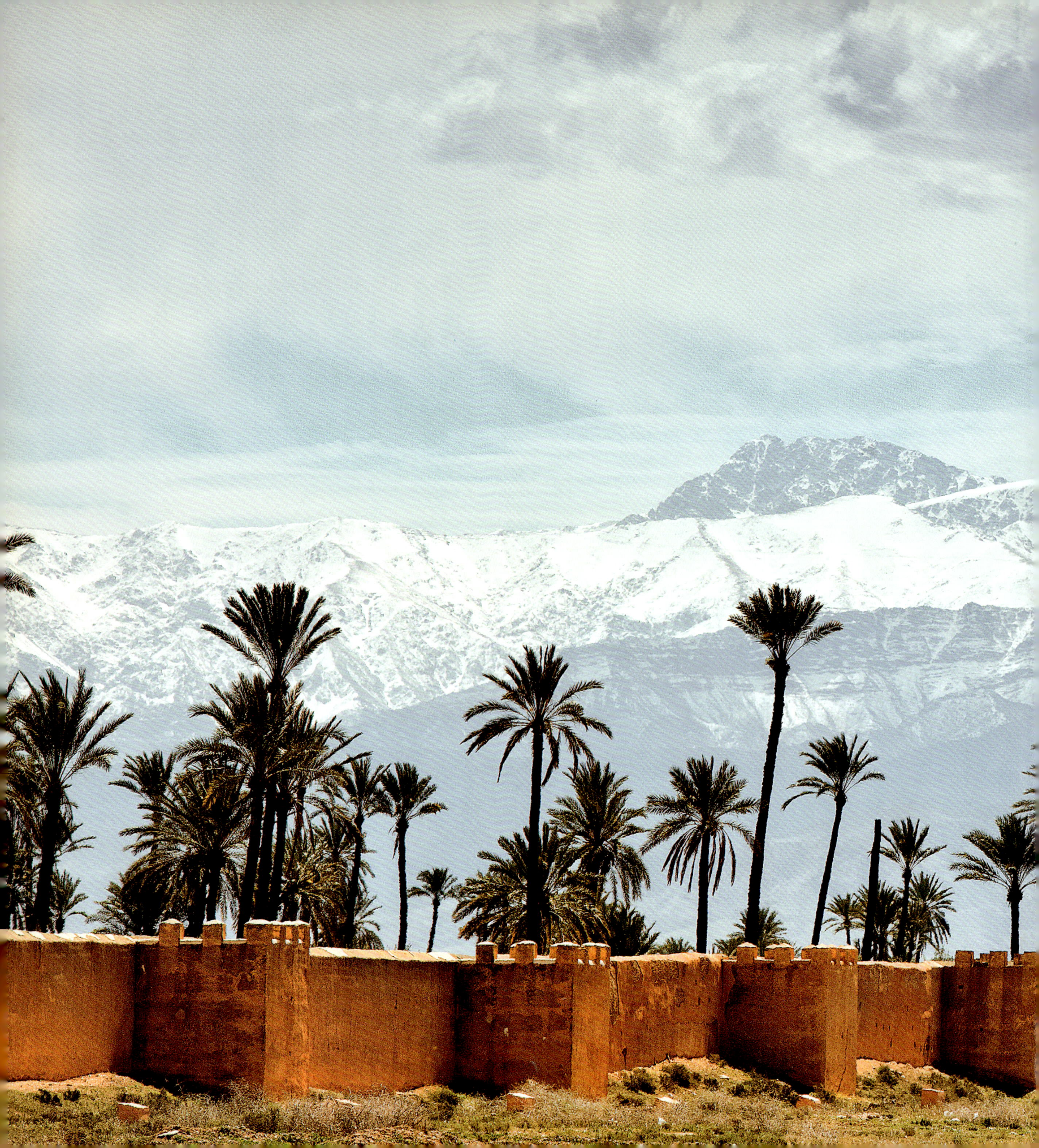

contents

Map 6
Introduction 7

1. The Agdal 14
2. The Menara 20
3. Gardens of the Koutoubia 26
4. The Badi Palace 30
5. The Bahia Palace 36
6. Dar Si Said 42
7. Riad Mounia 46
8. Riad Enija 50
9. Riad Madani 56
10. The Mamounia Gardens 62
11. Arsat Moulay Abdeslam Cyber Park 68
12. Jnane el Harti 74
13. Jardin Majorelle 80
14. The Palais Rhoul 88
15. Les Deux Tours 92
16. Jnane Tamsna 98
17. The Beldi Country Club 102
18. Gardens of the Musée de la Palmeraie 108
19. Amanjena 112
20. Ksar Char-Bagh 118

Visiting the Gardens 124
Glossary 126
Select Bibliography 126
`Acknowledgments 126
Index 127

Map of Marrakesh

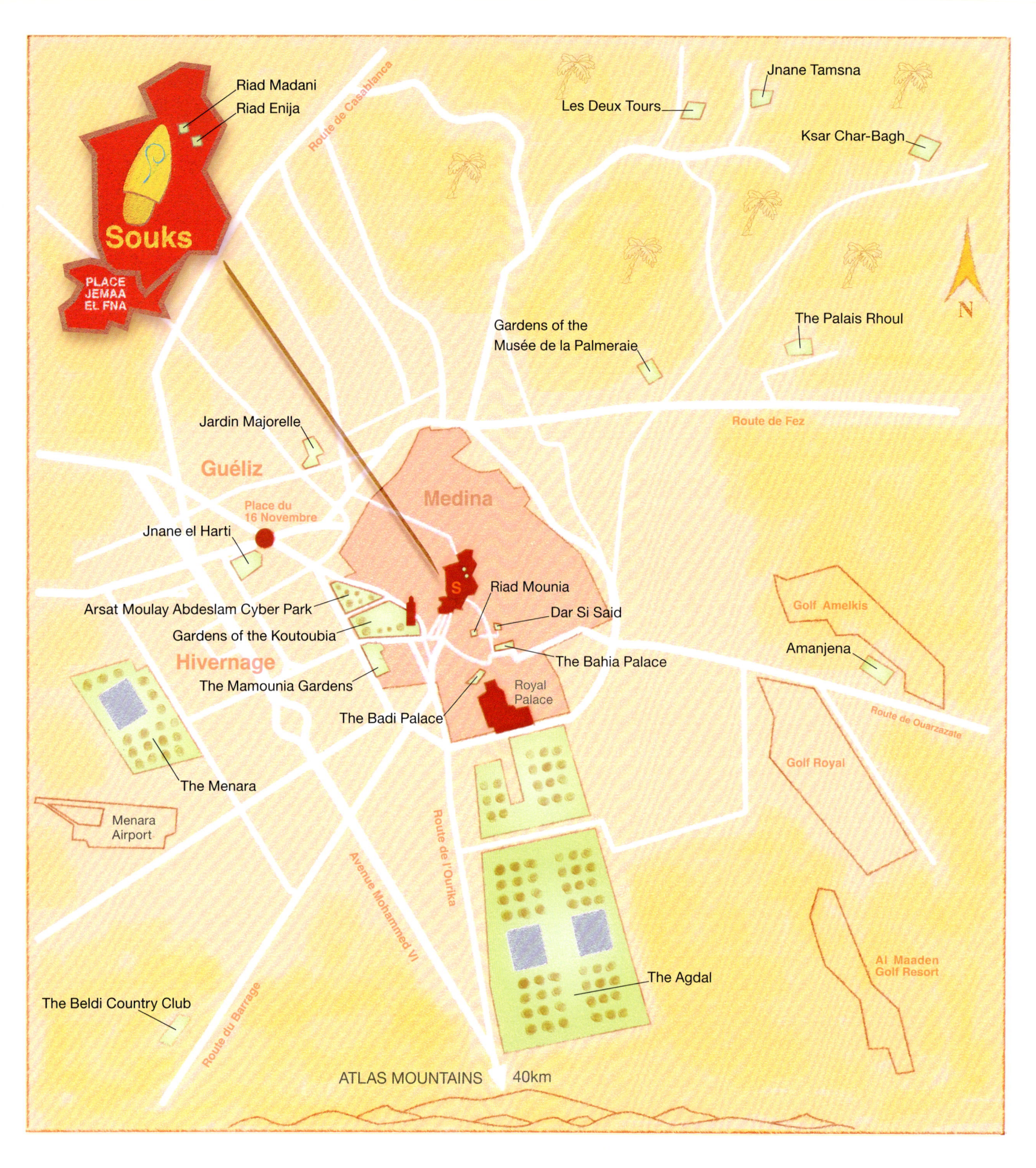

- Riad Madani
- Riad Enija
- **Souks**
- **PLACE JEMAA EL FNA**
- Jnane Tamsna
- Les Deux Tours
- Ksar Char-Bagh
- Route de Casablanca
- Gardens of the Musée de la Palmeraie
- The Palais Rhoul
- Jardin Majorelle
- Route de Fez
- **Guéliz**
- **Medina**
- Place du 16 Novembre
- Jnane el Harti
- Riad Mounia
- Arsat Moulay Abdeslam Cyber Park
- Dar Si Said
- Gardens of the Koutoubia
- **Hivernage**
- The Bahia Palace
- Golf Amelkis
- The Mamounia Gardens
- Amanjena
- The Badi Palace
- Royal Palace
- Route de Ouarzazate
- The Menara
- Golf Royal
- Menara Airport
- Route de l'Ourika
- Avenue Mohammed VI
- The Agdal
- Al Maaden Golf Resort
- The Beldi Country Club
- Route du Barrage
- ATLAS MOUNTAINS 40km

6 Gardens of Marrakesh

Introduction

Marrakesh has become a destination of choice for visitors seeking a taste of adventure and the exotic, twinned with a degree of sophistication and luxury. The city has all it needs to dazzle: a picture-book setting with views of the High Atlas Mountains, wonderful climate and cuisine, exotic sights, sounds and smells, great shopping, a warm and friendly people and nearly a thousand years of history.

Known as 'the rose among the palms', the city is characterised by its pink-coloured *pisé* (rammed earth) architecture and its deeply-rooted tradition for gardens and green spaces. Right from the start it was conceived as a garden city with orchards, market gardens and pleasure gardens as part of its urban model. Today this model is threatened by rampant development but there is a growing consciousness of the need to protect and exploit such a valuable garden heritage. The current king, Mohammed VI, has done much to raise expectations in this area and has put in place directives which aim to protect the environment and encourage new garden-making initiatives. With new projects, both private and public, springing up everywhere, the city is experiencing something of a garden renaissance.

Marrakesh is famous for its fabulous souks where shopping is an art, but it is above all a cultural destination with most visitors interested in exploring something of the life and history of the city. The majority of historic sites are inextricable from their gardens, or indeed are historic green spaces: the huge royal orchard pleasure gardens of the twelfth-century Agdal and Menara, the grand ruins of the sixteenth-century Badi Palace, the *riad* gardens of the late nineteenth-century Bahia Palace and the Dar Si Said Museum. The newcomer may be forgiven for imagining that the Arsat Moulay Abdeslam Cyber Park is a business centre for the IT industry, but it is in fact the juxtaposition of two historic gardens which have been carefully researched, using the latest archaeological techniques, and painstakingly restored.

Many tourists stay in hotels with splendid gardens. The most famous of these is perhaps the Mamounia Hotel which was created by the French in 1923 on the site of a nineteenth-century royal palace, incorporating nearly eight hectares of historic orchard gardens. Hotels and the tourist industry are one of the driving forces behind garden making today. Designers are at the cutting edge of a growing debate over whether there is a need to develop an authentic idiom which is rooted in local traditions or to adopt cultural norms which reflect creeping globalisation. Do European lawns and herbaceous borders really have a place in modern Marrakesh? A simple question, but one which acquires layers of meaning in the context of the city's history and ecology. The issues of tradition or modernity, the secular or spiritual and the local or international perhaps have to be answered in different ways for each of the city's three distinct districts: the Medina, the New Town, and the Palmery.

The Medina refers to the historic centre built within the city walls which were first raised in 1126–27 by the Almoravid sultan Ali ben Youssef. It has two beating hearts, one spiritual and one of more earthly delights: the beautiful square minaret of the twelfth-century Koutoubia Mosque is the dominant landmark of the city, and its surrounding gardens soak up the crowds after Friday prayer; just a short walk away is the historic Place Jemaa el-Fna, designated by UNESCO in 2001 as a 'Masterpiece of the Oral and Intangible Heritage of Humanity'. All life seems to be on show here: food stalls, women offering henna tattoos, young men displaying Barbary apes on chains, water sellers in colourful lampshade-like hats, storytellers, magicians, jugglers, snake charmers, musicians, singers and pedlars of curious-looking traditional medicines. The dichotomy between private, spiritual life and the hurly-burly of public life is an important aspect of understanding Marrakesh, including one of its most famous phenomena, the *riad*.

The term *riad* refers to a relatively large planted urban garden, classically enclosed on all sides, and incorporating domestic buildings and walls. These courtyard gardens are an expression of a whole way of life and have a long and rich cultural identity associated with Islamic thought on the nature of paradise and the privacy of family. They were designed to be a private haven where nature heals the troubled soul of the responsibilities of life outside the sanctuary of the home. Many urban dwellers in the great cities of the West are increasingly interested in the restorative quality of nature, and as such the *riad* model has much to offer. However, the term *riad* has been appropriated and given a wider significance and now needs to have its original meaning restored. The 1970s saw the beginning of a trend for Europeans to buy up houses in the Medina and turn them into guesthouses. Some of these had authentic *riad* gardens but others were simply *dars*, or houses, with paved patio courtyards. The distinction between these two began to be blurred so that *riad* came to be understood as an exotic architectural phenomenon, romantic, glamorous and luxurious, where visitors could experience an Arabian Nights sojourn. It is time for historic *riad* gardens to be re-evaluated as highly designed spaces with an important intellectual and spiritual content.

The *riad* is one authentic model for designers to consider; another, which is also pertinent, is the *arset* or *arsat*. These were productive, irrigated gardens on a relatively modest scale often intended to

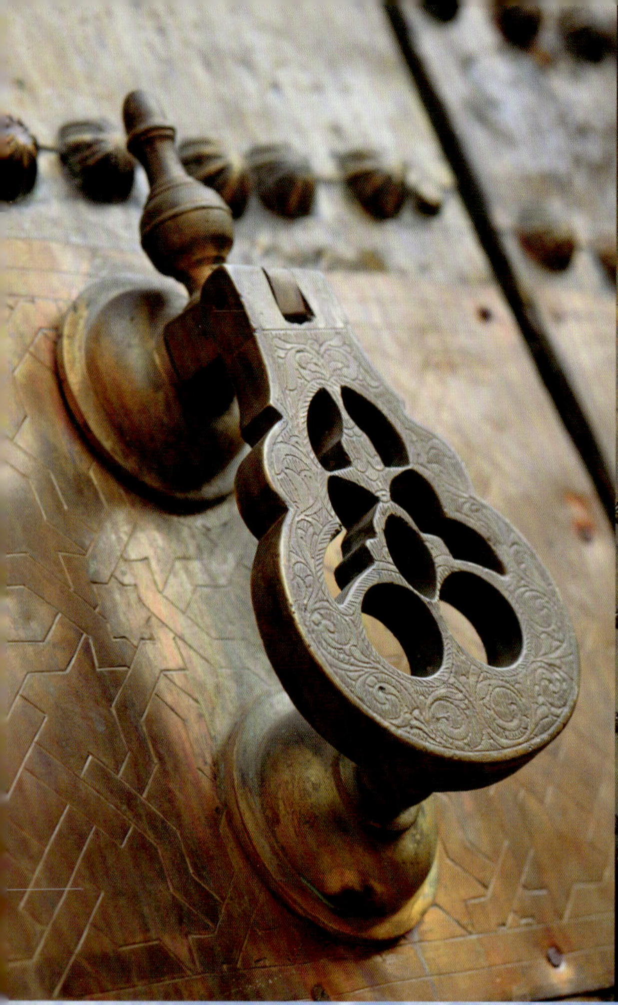
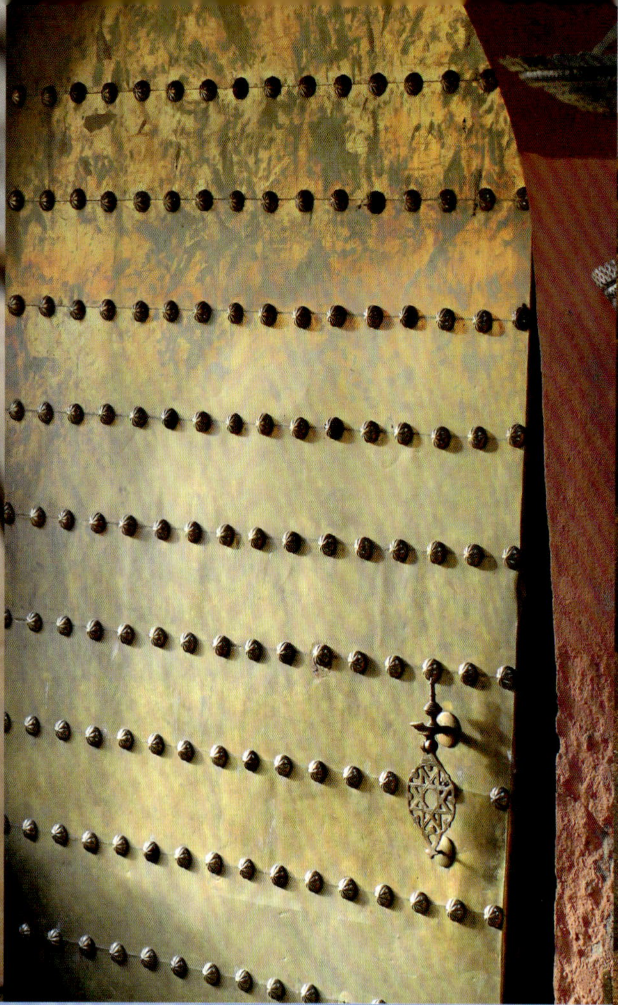
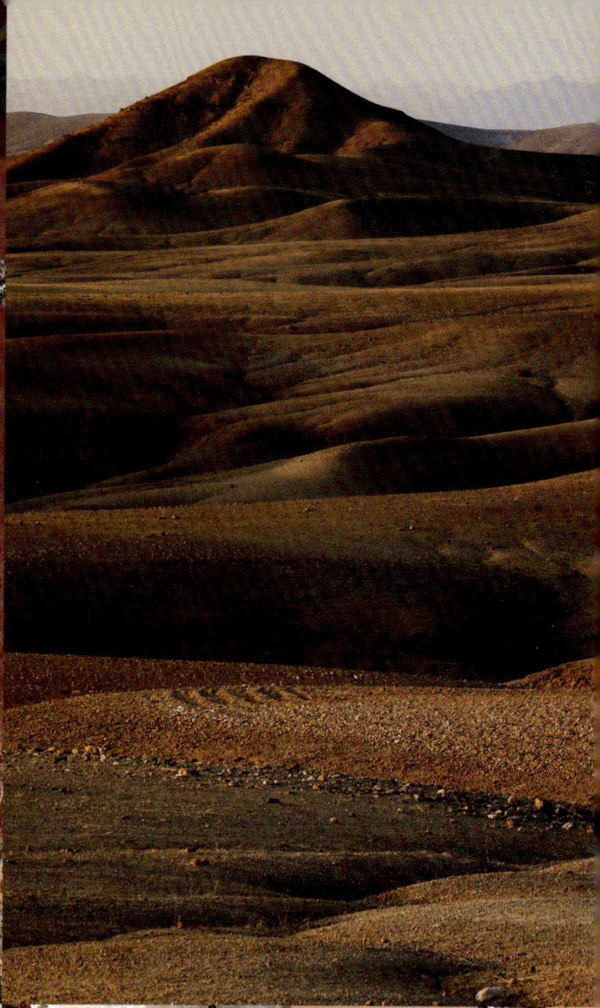
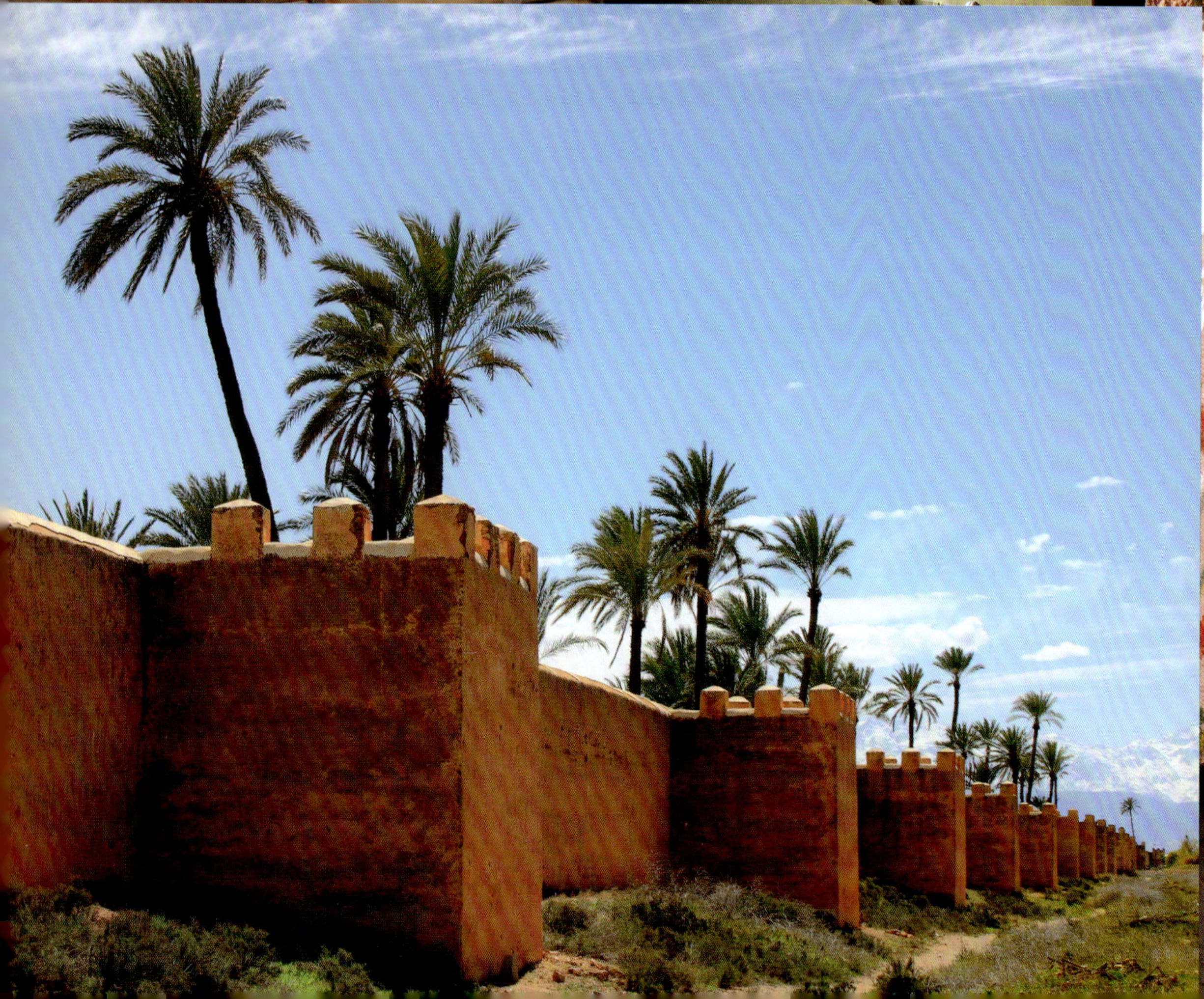
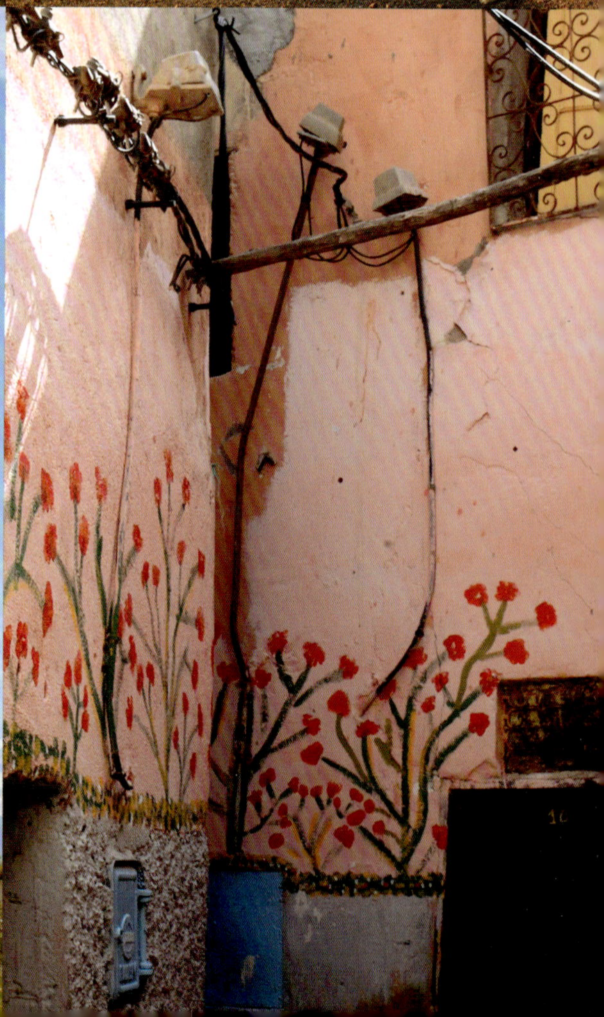

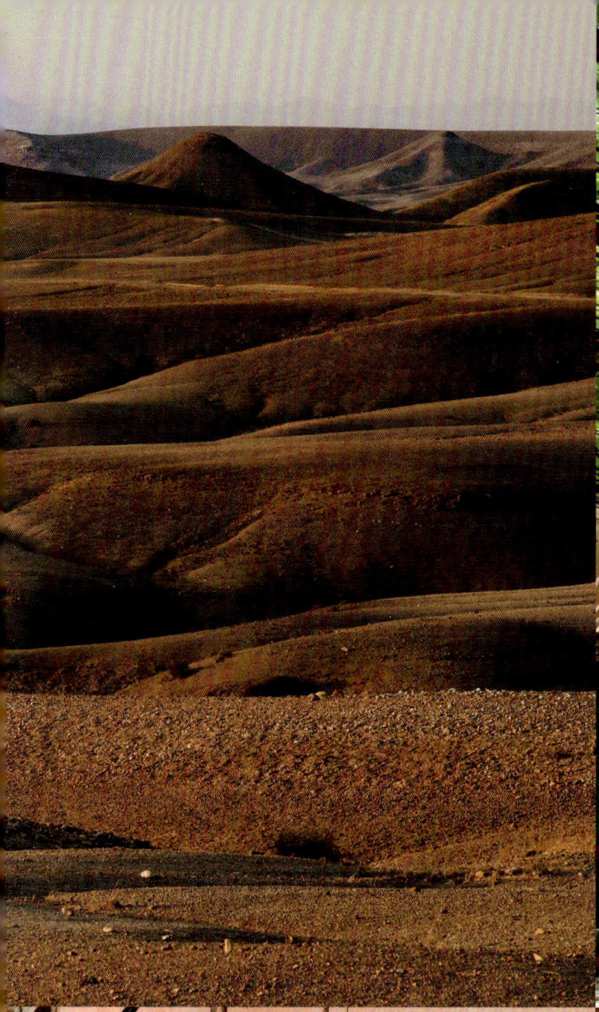
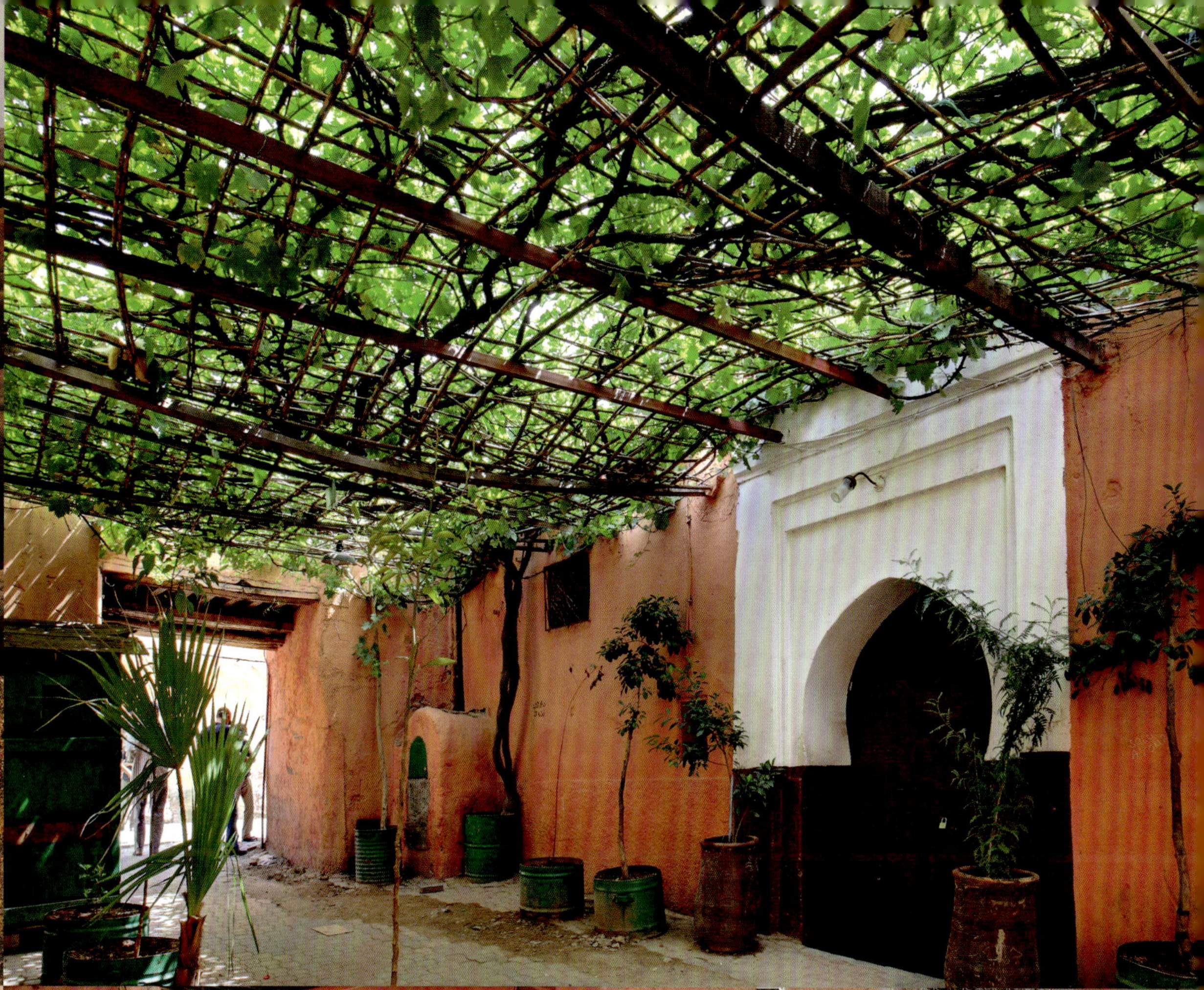
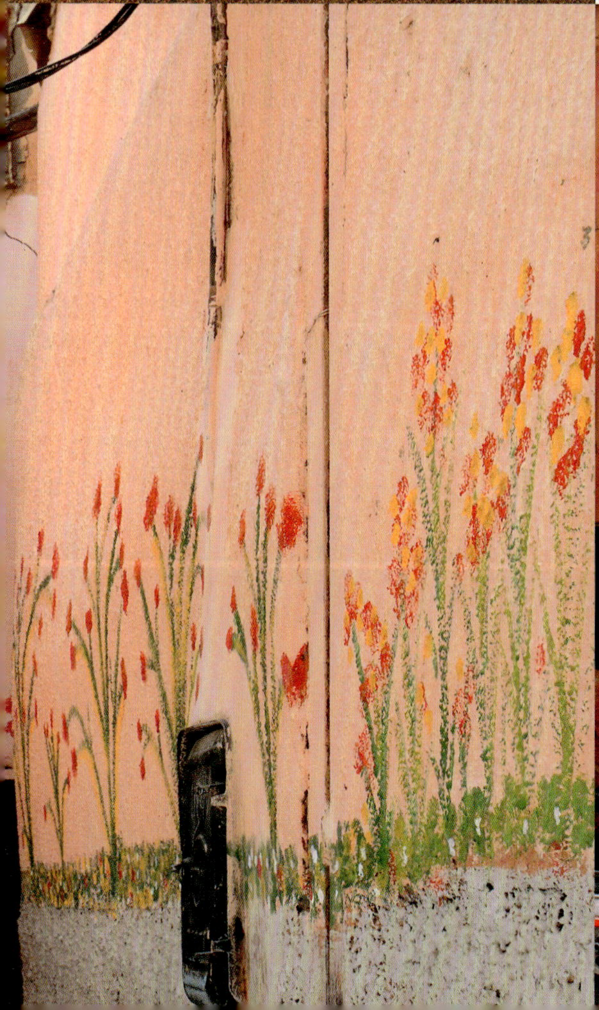
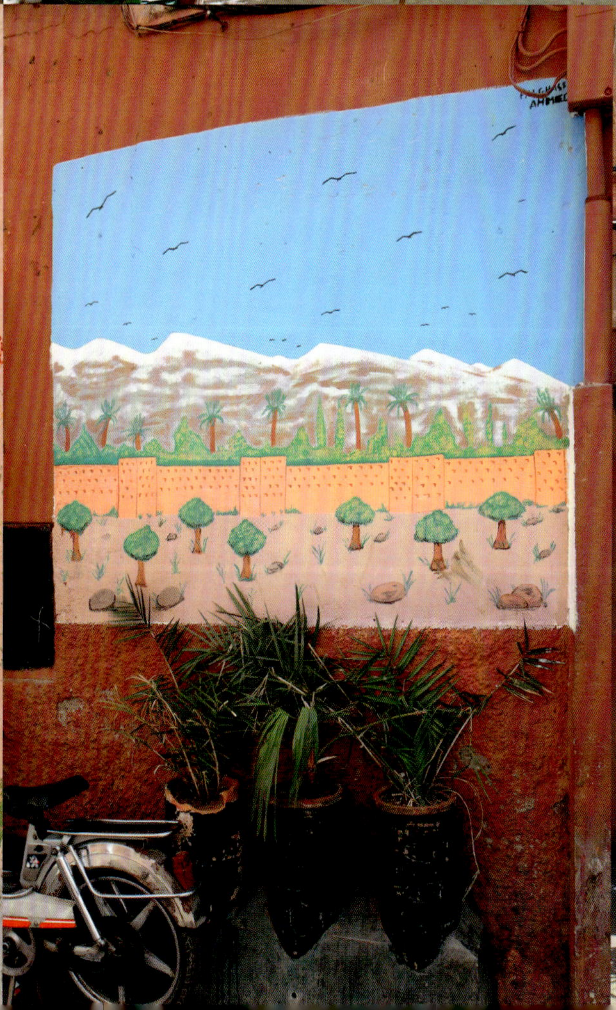
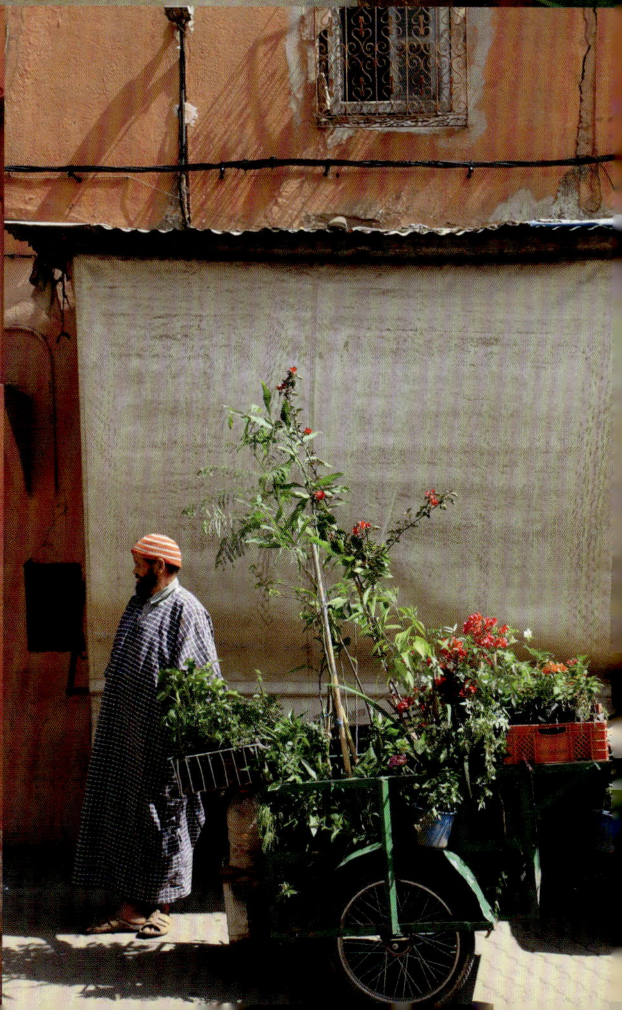

double as pleasure gardens. There were many of these *arsats* arranged around the interior of the city walls right up until the 1950s. They existed as part of the great concentric rings of market gardens and orchards which surrounded the city from medieval times, and were particularly useful in the past as a source of fresh food when the city was under siege. Modern concerns over the quality and ecological soundness of our cities' food chains have given rise to the urban farm phenomenon. Individuals are also increasingly subscribing to the 'grow your own' movement. Vegetables in urban gardens are grown to satisfy a basic emotional need to be in touch with nature as well as providing a source of food. Thus the boundary between pleasure and utility is being challenged. It would be perverse of garden designers in Marrakesh to ignore a garden tradition which has addressed this concept for centuries.

Marrakesh was planned as an oasis of green set with cubes of pink dwellings. This model of a garden city was still evident in 1912 when 60 square metres of green space per inhabitant was the norm as opposed to the derisory two square metres today. Something is being done to redress this problem thanks to the pioneering work of individuals such as Mohammed El Faïz, who first raised the alarm. Historic gardens are receiving the government attention they merit, and there are many small projects working to bring green back into the thick of the souks with potted plants, traditional *daliya* (vines trained on trellis for shade) and tiny plant nurseries based around the water points associated with mosques. The Medina is the old heart of the modern city which still works within the context of an Islamic way of life. When the French took control of Marrakesh during the Protectorate in 1912 they decreed that the Medina should be kept intact and developed a separate area for themselves outside the city walls – the New Town.

The New Town consists of two adjacent areas: the Guéliz, which means little hill, to the north west and the Hivernage, a later garden suburb developed to the south of the Guéliz. An axial road, the current Avenue Mohammed V, was driven from the Koutoubia Mosque straight out to the heart of the Guéliz where Europeans created an expatriate way of life. This separation from the values and aesthetic of the Medina is palpable today. Streets are wide, tree-lined avenues, with luxury apartments and glass-fronted shops selling familiar brands. There are discos, bars and clubs and gaggles of young people dressed in the latest Western fashions. The French established residential areas of villa-style houses surrounded by gardens modelled on those they had back home. After Independence in 1956 many wealthier young Moroccan families moved here to escape the heavy burden of duty and obligation which the traditional values of life in the Medina imposed on them.

The colonists gardened in their familiar idioms but were obliged to adapt their plant palette to the climate. Clipped pomegranate and plumbago replaced the box and yew topiary of formal French gardens. Avenues of jacaranda, orange trees and pruned olives were substituted for the familiar plane trees of Paris. Swathes of green lawn, brightly-coloured bedding schemes and swimming pools helped the newcomers feel at home. At the same time there was a certain romance associated with the exoticism of the region. The early Protectorate years coincided with a period of botanical bonanza with many new species arriving in Europe from across the world. Marvels which required a hothouse elsewhere thrived naturally in this semi-arid climate, allowing enthusiasts greater creative freedom. One such enthusiast was Jacques Majorelle whose eponymous garden in the New Town is an enchanting example of this phenomenon.

Many Moroccan contemporary landscape designers are trained in France or the United States. Some people express a concern that they have been inculcated with the same Eurocentric, domineering approach to nature and garden design which informed the colonial-style gardens of the New Town. However, there are significant numbers of people interested in making gardens which reconcile respect for the environment, sensitivity to cultural models and the desire to be of their time. These ideas are being tested in the gardens of prestige hotels, clubs and wealthy private owners in the outskirts of the city and the Palmery.

The Palmery has long been one of the wonders of Marrakesh, a thick green crescent of luxuriant palm trees stretching from the city walls to the river Issil in the north east. No one really knows the origin of this legendary palm grove but a popular myth ascribes it to Berber tribesmen carelessly discarding the stones of eaten dates around their encampment. Whatever the truth of this tale, what is certain is that the Palmery was an important green lung of the city providing both economic and recreational benefits. The palms were tended by peasants living in small, scattered hamlets called *douars*. These were skilled agricultural workers who tended crops grown in the shade of the trees. They kept the traditional watering systems functioning and ensured that trees which were not able to access water from the water table were irrigated. People from the city used the Palmery as a recreational area, a space in which to experience *bayha* or felicity. In this sense the whole Palmery was a park, an agricultural landscape which also touched the sensibilities of the population.

PREVIOUS PAGES The arid, almost monochromatic landscape around Marrakesh fuels the desire to escape to the safety and luxury of a cool, verdant, walled garden – even if you have to paint one yourself.

RIGHT The beautiful pink earthen walls surrounding the Medina seem to glow and change colour at different times of day. Sections are adorned with public planting, as here where olive trees have been clipped to form living sculptures.

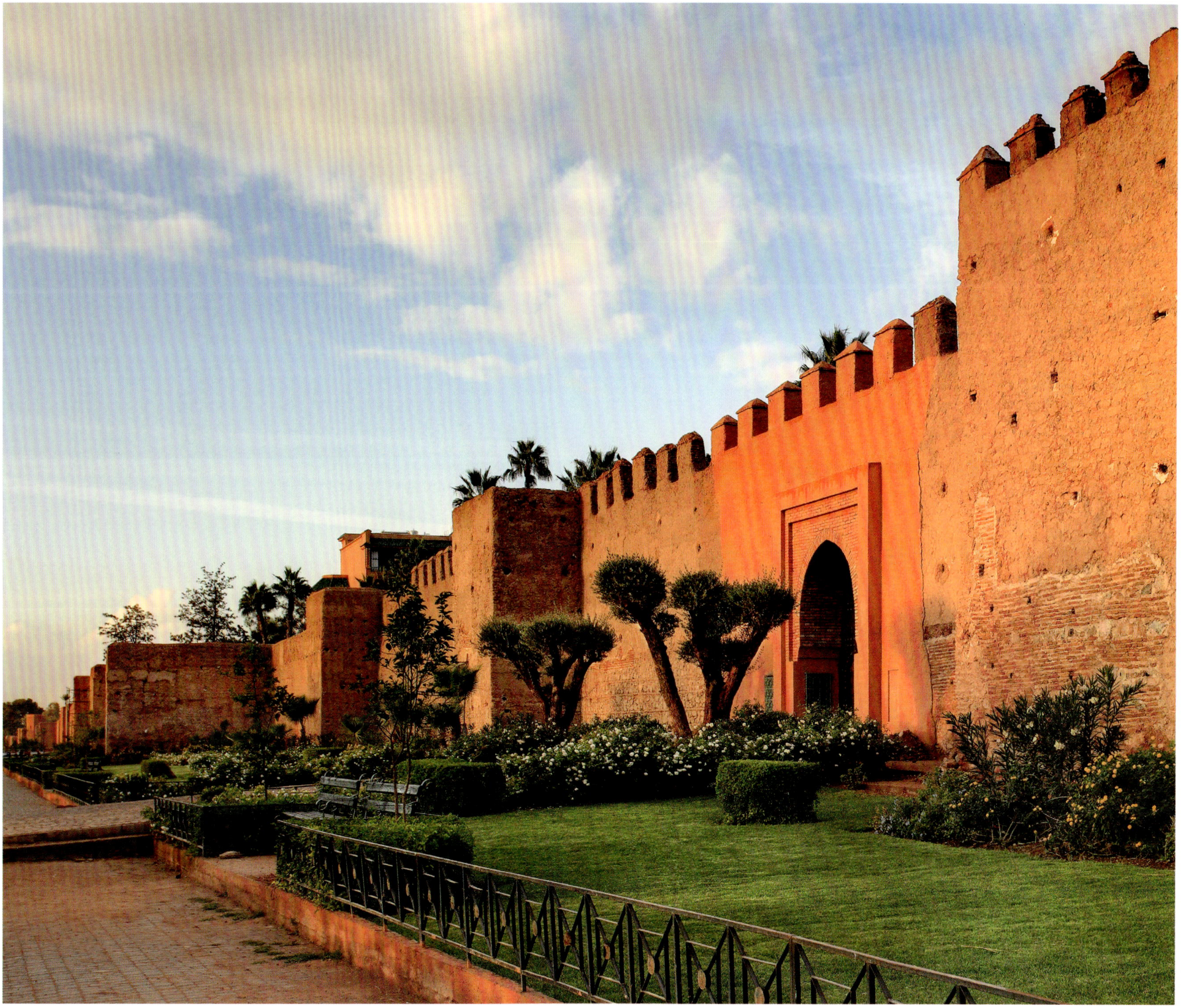

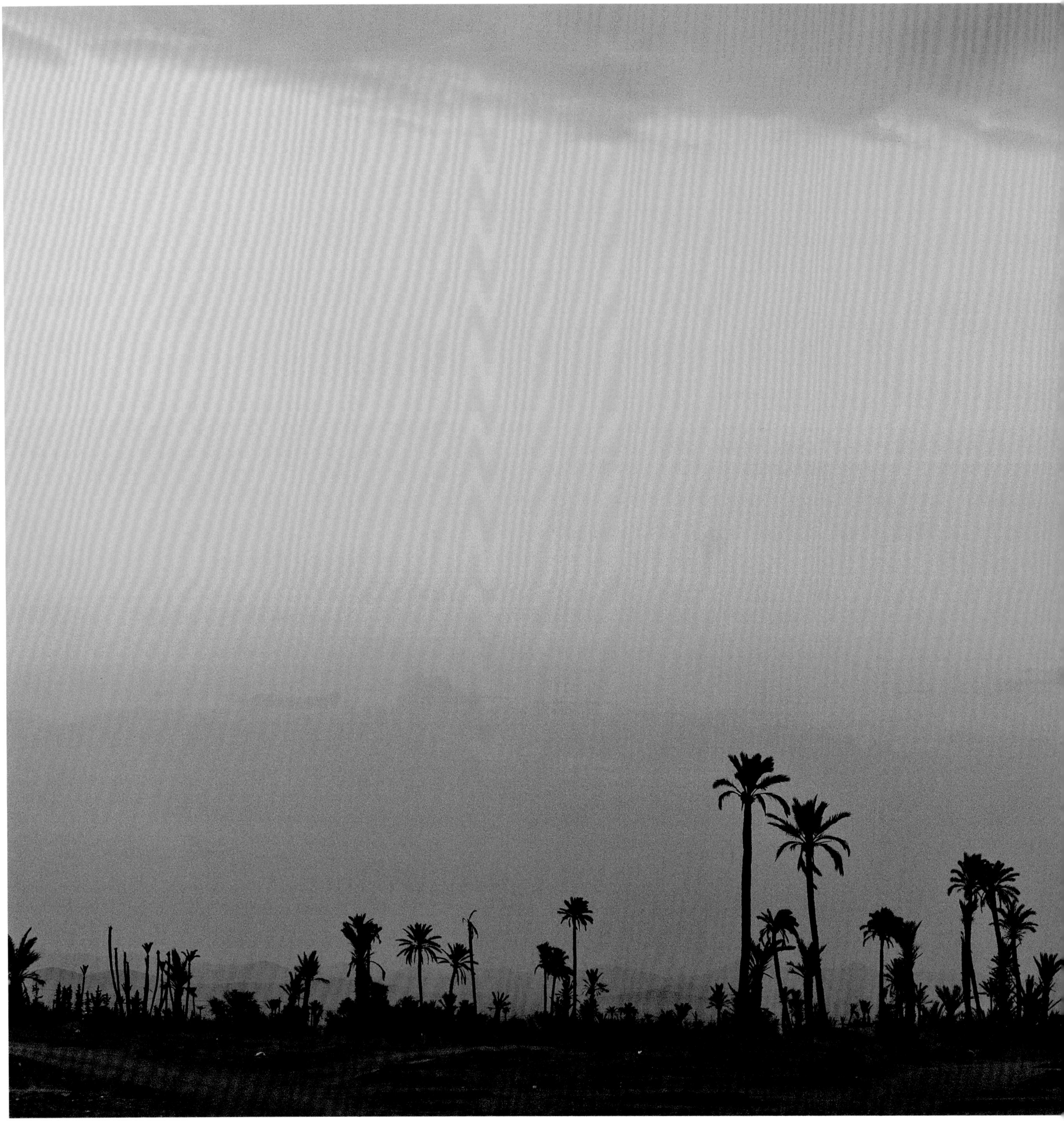

This great natural resource was protected in 1929 by a *dahir*, or local decree. Nevertheless, the extent of the Palmery has shrunk drastically and its beauty has suffered for a combination of reasons: local populations have been drawn to higher wages in other industries leaving the groves untended; date palms (*Phoenix dactylifera*) have been devastated by the deadly Bayoud disease; and there are an increasing number of development projects. Some of these problems are being addressed; a massive replanting scheme involving thousands of new, disease-resistant specimens is under way. Building regulations are being tightened, and rules enforced about replacing any trees removed during construction work. Despite the problems the Palmery is still an attractive place to live and has gained the reputation of being the Hollywood of Marrakesh with its many celebrity residents.

The main feature of life in the Palmery is space. Plots have by law to be at least one hectare in size and many are much larger. The architectural strictures of the Medina do not apply and styles are wide ranging, often fantastic, with gardens to match. The contrast between the now dry, stressed landscape of the Palmery and these luxuriant gardens is astonishing, making it easy to imagine the sensation of a desert traveller entering an oasis. Such gardens in these climatic conditions are, however, expensive and several individuals with interesting ideas have opened their homes to tourism as a way of sustaining their projects. One such is Gary Martin whose edible landscape garden at the Jnane Tamsna is a fascinating alternative aesthetic which contrasts with the Greco-Roman fantasy garden of the nearby Palais Rhoul or the gentle village-inspired gardens of Les Deux Tours.

There is much to surprise and delight in the gardens of Marrakesh. The city is buzzing with new ideas and projects aimed at improving public spaces. On the short drive from the airport to the city centre I complimented my driver on the delightful public planting which lined our route. 'Yes', he gravely replied, 'we are working to beautify our city – like that.' He pointed to a sole palm tree, unusually tall and straight but otherwise unremarkable, until he laughingly explained that it was in fact a telecommunications post – in disguise. Who could fail to be enchanted?

The individual gardens that follow are grouped together to correspond with the three geographical categories discussed above and are also, broadly speaking, in chronological order.

LEFT Sunset in the Palmery is a moment of eerie beauty with the architectural forms of *Phoenix dactylifera* in silhouette as far as the eye can see.

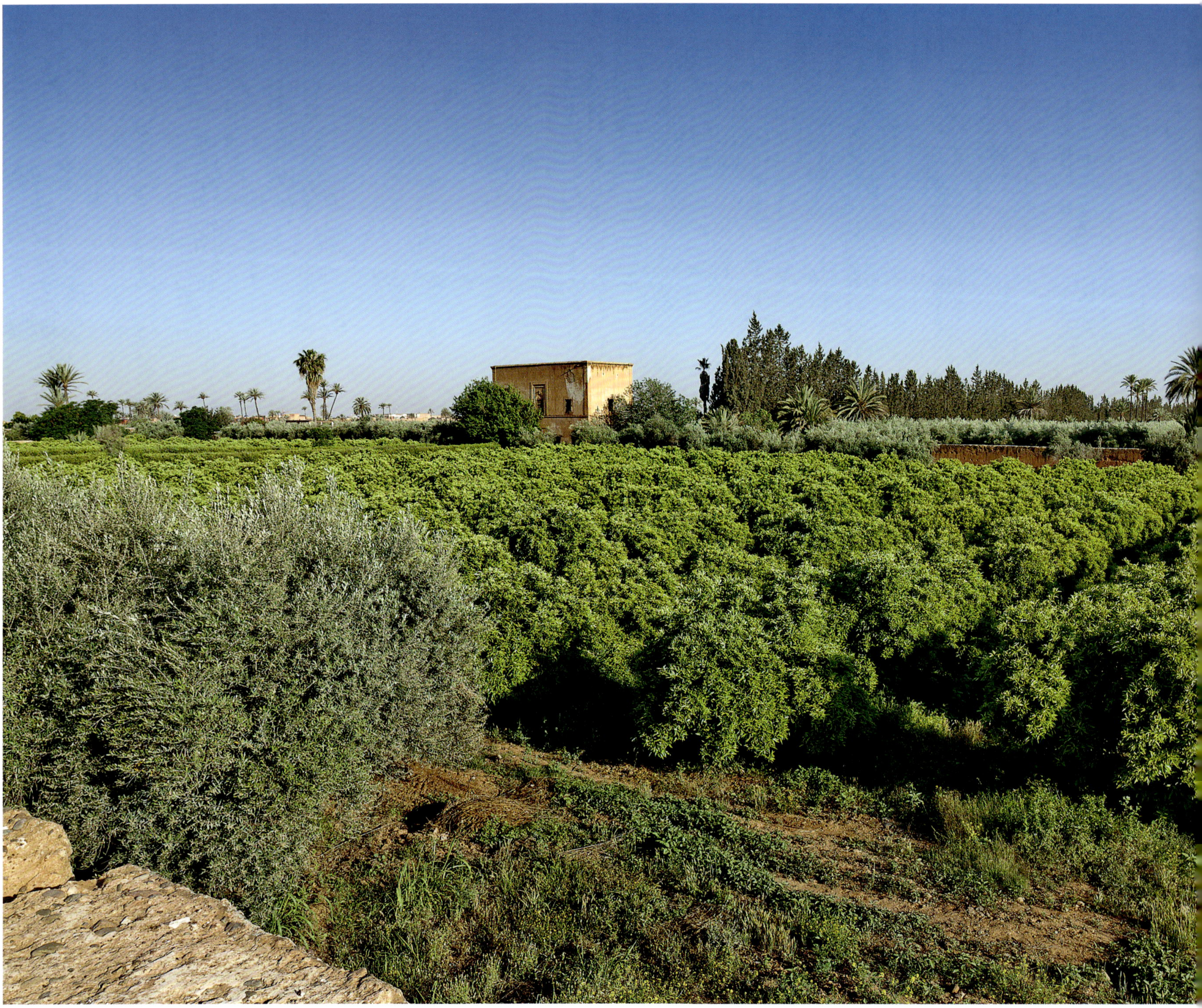

1. The Agdal

LEFT The sheer size of this huge, productive pleasure garden is hard to imagine. Walled orchards of thirsty citrus trees, such as the orange grove seen here, were placed near the irrigation basin. Less needy olives appear as a band of silver beyond, with a line of cypress marking an important vista.

The Agdal is the most important garden in Marrakesh. Huge in its expanse and over 800 years old, it is sometimes referred to as the Islamic Versailles. A tiny part of it is open to the public twice weekly, on Fridays and Sundays, when people come to feed the monstrously large carp in the ancient water basin, picnic under the olive trees and, on a clear day in winter, admire the spectacular view of the snow-capped Atlas Mountains against a pristine blue sky. Marrakshis seem to have a natural affection for this iconic site belonging to their king but for the foreign visitor getting to grips with an unfamiliar garden type requires a bit more effort.

The Agdal was a vast productive royal pleasure garden made by Sultan Abd el Moumen (r.1130–63), along with its sister garden the Menara, in around 1156/7. El Moumen had captured the city from the founding Almoravids in 1147 and was the first of a new and dynamic dynasty, the Almohads, who made Marrakesh their capital, bequeathing it fine architecture and a taste for the arts. It was also important for the new king to demonstrate his power by securing a plentiful water supply and a good source of fresh food. His plan for an impressive designed landscape, covering around 500 hectares to the south of the Medina and the royal palace, combined both imperatives in a new way which was to become the template for a fundamental garden type, the Islamic *agdal*-garden. Water, fruit, perfumed blooms and comfort were of primary concern. However, unlike the typical, inward-looking, Islamic Paradise garden, the Agdal reached out towards the greater landscape, appropriating natural features and creating lines of perspective, centuries before any European garden did the same. It is an aesthetic born of the arid conditions of the region, the agricultural practices devised to combat these conditions and the desert nomad's dream of a cool, well watered, fruitful oasis.

The garden was originally named El Buhayra, literally 'little sea' in Arabic, but became known as the Agdal in the seventeenth century, after the Berber word which refers to a riverside meadow enclosed by a stone wall. The site is surrounded by nine kilometres of rammed earth walls, punctuated by *borj*, fortified towers, which are contiguous with the city itself. Inside these walls the land is divided into large plots arranged on a grid system, with wide paths edged by a single file of olive trees. These areas are subdivided into a chequerboard of smaller plots, each planted with a single species of productive trees such as oranges, lemons and other citrus, walnuts, olives, almonds, figs and pomegranates. Large tracts were reserved for grape vines too, as well as the multi-functional date palm and seasonal vegetables of every type. There is even evidence of experimental trials with new varieties, making this a garden open to innovation and therefore an important element of the economic life of the city. These sections were embroidered together by borders of fragrant shrubs such as myrtle, honeysuckle, jasmine and elderberry or trelliswork with trained roses. Records state that the many thousands of trees comprising the entire 500 hectares of orchards were planted in a single day by a veritable 'tide of humanity'.

All this incredible planting would have been useless without an impressive supply of water. The previous dynasty had brought water from the base of the Atlas Mountains, a distance of over thirty kilometres, using an ancient design of subterranean channels known as *khettara*. The brilliant architect and hydraulic engineer, Al-Haj Yaish, is thought to be the genius behind the design of the Agdal, including the two huge, elevated reservoirs which dominate

BELOW The Tank of Health was one of two irrigation basins which were designed with both utility and pleasure in mind. Unfortunately for Sultan Mohammed IV it proved to be very unhealthy. He drowned in its waters in 1873 while out boating with his son. His epitaph is pragmatic: 'He departed this life in a water tank, in the expectation of something better to come'.

BELOW LEFT The gardens are still irrigated using the original hydraulic system which harnessed gravity to supply a network of channels with water from the raised tank.

BELOW RIGHT The monstrous looking carp which live in the tank put on a popular horror show for the price of a few bits of stale bread. Wily young boys have been known to get a free performance by offering up stones tied to a string.

The Agdal 17

the central portion of the site. To the east, the Sahrij el-Gharsyya is notable for its central island which was designed as an optical illusion so that trees seemed to grow directly out of the water. The larger of the two tanks, measuring 205m x 180m, lies to the west and is known as the Sahrij el-Hana (Tank of Health). It is this basin which is currently on view to the public, and while its muddy waters might not look so healthy today, it is still an impressive sight. It must have been daunting to the military personnel who were taught to swim here in the twelfth century before being shipped over to Andalusia. These tanks were intended to be beautiful and enjoyable, a source of fun and entertainment, but crucially their main purpose was to irrigate the garden. Planting was arranged in a hierarchy of need so water-loving citrus were planted in enclosures nearest the tanks, with olives giving way to vines which require very little water. The drop from water level down to the gardens below is quite pronounced and everywhere there is evidence of the complicated gravity-fed irrigation system which criss-crossed the site. The basins also fed numerous ornamental fountains and smaller pools which were often sited near little pavilions and kiosks throughout the garden.

The design of the Agdal or Buhayra was a success story which was repeated throughout Morocco and beyond to Gibraltar and Seville. The gardens were marvelled at for their prodigious productivity, their physical beauty and their great expanses of water – amplified by their context in a land where drought and hardship were never distant. Records show that in 1170 the Agdal provided enough *rob*, a sweet liqueur cut with water, to satisfy 45,000 thirsty guests at a tribal meeting. A project of this magnitude was a status symbol which required great political will and power and in this respect it bears comparison with the creation of Louis XIV's palace at Versailles. Another obvious similarity is the importance of perspective in its design but essentially these are two very different gardens. At Versailles it is the magnificence of the architecture which is at the heart of the design with the garden being an extension of the power of Louis XIV over all living things. While the Agdal was undoubtedly a symbol of royal power and prestige, it did not seek to dominate nature with clippers or to divide its gifts into prosaic edibles and rarefied blooms. The garden is a place of joy in its own right with everything designed to be both useful and to give pleasure and

18 Gardens of Marrakesh

LEFT The Agdal is enclosed by nine kilometres of *pisé* walls. Here a section is being repaired using sun-dried, adobe bricks made from local red earth mixed with straw.

ABOVE Rows of old olive trees create shade and a bucolic atmosphere, which is much appreciated by local families who come here to picnic, relax and escape the frenzy of city life.

delight to all the senses, there being no conflict in the two branches of horticulture. Nature is presented at its most welcoming, as an oasis of comfort for the weary desert traveller.

Today the garden, which was listed in 1985 as an UNESCO World Heritage Site, is being carefully studied by a range of relevant experts, including some involved in the historic gardens of southern Spain. The intention is to undertake a painstaking restoration project in the coming years which will reveal the true nature of this amazing garden, one of the oldest surviving in the Arab Islamic world.

20 Gardens of Marrakesh

2. The Menara

Everyone in Marrakesh loves the Menara. People come here to enjoy a stroll around the cooling waters of its expansive irrigation tank, do a bit of jogging, or picnic in the shade of the olive groves. Outside the gate there is usually a cluster of camels waiting patiently to take nervous novices for a ride, while nearby a few stallholders dedicate themselves to making the visitor-experience more pleasurable, supplying drinks, hats, and, on occasion, umbrellas. Some people, however, come here to hunt. Loaded with camera equipment they patiently stalk the photographer's holy grail, an iconic composition of water, romantic pavilion, regal cypress and snow-capped mountain, all bathed in a magical late-afternoon light.

The Menara is little sister to the Agdal, similar in its design but smaller, 98 hectares against 500, and less varied in its planting. Both gardens were developed around 1156/7 as part of an ambitious programme of improvement envisaged for the city by Sultan Abd el Moumen. Not content merely to emulate conventions of the past, El Moumen engendered a new garden type, the *agdal*, which sought to innovate in terms of conception, with an emphasis on scale and perspective. The basic blueprint is that of a productive pleasure garden, incorporating a large body of water, surrounded by plots of orchards and edible plants. However, this seemingly prescribed model immediately produced two gardens which have their own special character and inspired a variety of versions throughout the land and beyond into Andalusia. Sited to the south-west, the Menara lies two kilometres from the old city walls and exploits the natural panorama of the Atlas Mountains to the south and the arid hills of the Djebilet to the north. Originally a road led directly from the royal palace in the Medina, through a gate in the city walls known as the Bab el-Mahzan right up to the entrance of the garden. This road, city gate and palace complex were all destroyed in the thirteenth century at the fall of the Almohad dynasty but the garden survived because the Islamic faith forbade the destruction of nature, changing the pre-Islamic habit of laying waste to swathes of productive land in time of war. Today the Avenue de la Menara goes some way to restoring the original intention.

LEFT This iconic view of the Menara, set against the Atlas, is eloquent evidence that the twelfth-century landscape architects were masters of their art. Appropriation of the landscape beyond the garden shows that Islamic designs were perfectly capable of being grand and outward looking.

LEFT The Menara is popular with Marrakshis and is a good spot for purveyors of ice-cream, hats, T-shirts, cold drinks and camel rides. Far from detracting from the scene their colourful stalls add a festive note to the garden gates.

BELOW LEFT Most visitors choose to stay near the basin and pavilion but the Menara has much more to offer. Stray a little way off the beaten track, especially at harvest time and the garden really reveals itself with wide paths, olive groves punctuated by palms and self-seeded natives, and a network of old irrigation channels.

RIGHT It is well worth paying the small entrance fee to visit the lovely pavilion built by Sultan Sidi Mohammed in 1866.

22 Gardens of Marrakesh

As in the Agdal, water is a crucial element in the design of the Menara, ensuring both profit and pleasure. The central feature of the garden is a reservoir measuring 195m x 160m, constructed above ground level in order to feed the irrigation system entirely by gravity. A short flight of steps leads up to the water's edge which is surrounded by a generous terrace where young and old alike dreamily perform endless circuits while chatting and snacking. Spread all around is a geometric carpet of grey-green olive trees laid out in strict order, each plot dissected by ten metre wide paths and channels of flowing water. Unlike the Agdal the planting is pretty much a monoculture, although it is punctuated by date palms and the odd horticultural intruder. Forty varieties of olive are grown here on a commercial basis and around the month of October straw-hatted workers move their ladders methodically through the groves handpicking the fruit as it ripens. It is a romantic sight, except for the stacks of modern, white plastic crates which have replaced the natural beauty of hand-woven baskets.

On the southern edge of the great basin lies a lovely pavilion, or *menzeh*, built by Sultan Sidi Mohammed in 1866 as a replacement for a previous building, probably dating from the sixteenth century. Surrounded by its own lushly planted walled garden the pavilion, which measures just 12m x 12m, was used by the sultans and some favoured courtiers as a private retreat from the public world. It is worth paying the entrance fee to view the site from the elevated position of the upper storey rooms and loggia, as the entire design is revealed from there. Seen from the balconied first floor terrace overlooking the basin the garden appears rather like a geometric diagram drawn on a giant blackboard. The rectangular reservoir sits in a larger rectangle filled with smaller quadrilateral olive groves, and the whole figure is bisected lengthwise by a wide avenue which seems to point a very long finger out into the landscape. Turning right towards the city one sees the other defining axis, this time linking the garden with that beacon of Marrakesh, the minaret of the Koutoubia Mosque. It is thought that this connection gives the garden its name as *menara* in Arabic can mean minaret. Look through a window on the south face and the bisecting avenue, lined with stately cypress, points to a backdrop of the Atlas Mountains. The Menara contradicts the Islamic tradition which favours designs which gently unfold. Unlike the Agdal it is small enough to be understood almost at a glance and its connection with the wider landscape is obvious.

Sultan Moulay Ismail (r.1672–1727) cherished the desire to extend this connection metaphorically as far as the court of France. In 1689 he fell madly in love with Marie Anne, Princess of Conti, the eldest (and favourite) daughter of Louis XIV, just from seeing her portrait. Convinced of his desirability, he dispatched the famous corsair Ben Aicha to France to arrange their marriage, only to receive a negative reply from the lady. She politely explained that she was a rare and precious flower, too used to the gardens of her father, who would undoubtedly die if uprooted and transplanted to a foreign soil. Not able to take a hint Moulay Ismail, from his capital Meknes, sought out the most beautiful garden in the kingdom as a suitable repository for his delicate bloom. Settling on the Menara he ordered its prettification to be fit for his foreign love. When supplicated a second time the princess gave a less floral reply. Heartbroken, the sultan is said to have planted two cypresses in memory of the passion he had hoped would flourish there. Fortunately his spirit recovered quickly enough – by the time of his death he is reputed to have sired around 800 children.

BELOW The architecture of the basin itself has been kept simple and somewhat austere, apart from details such as this shell-shaped water chute.

RIGHT The terrace of the pavilion provides a great viewing platform from where the overall geometry of the design can be appreciated, as well as the sightline which extends from the garden all the way to the minaret of the Koutoubia Mosque.

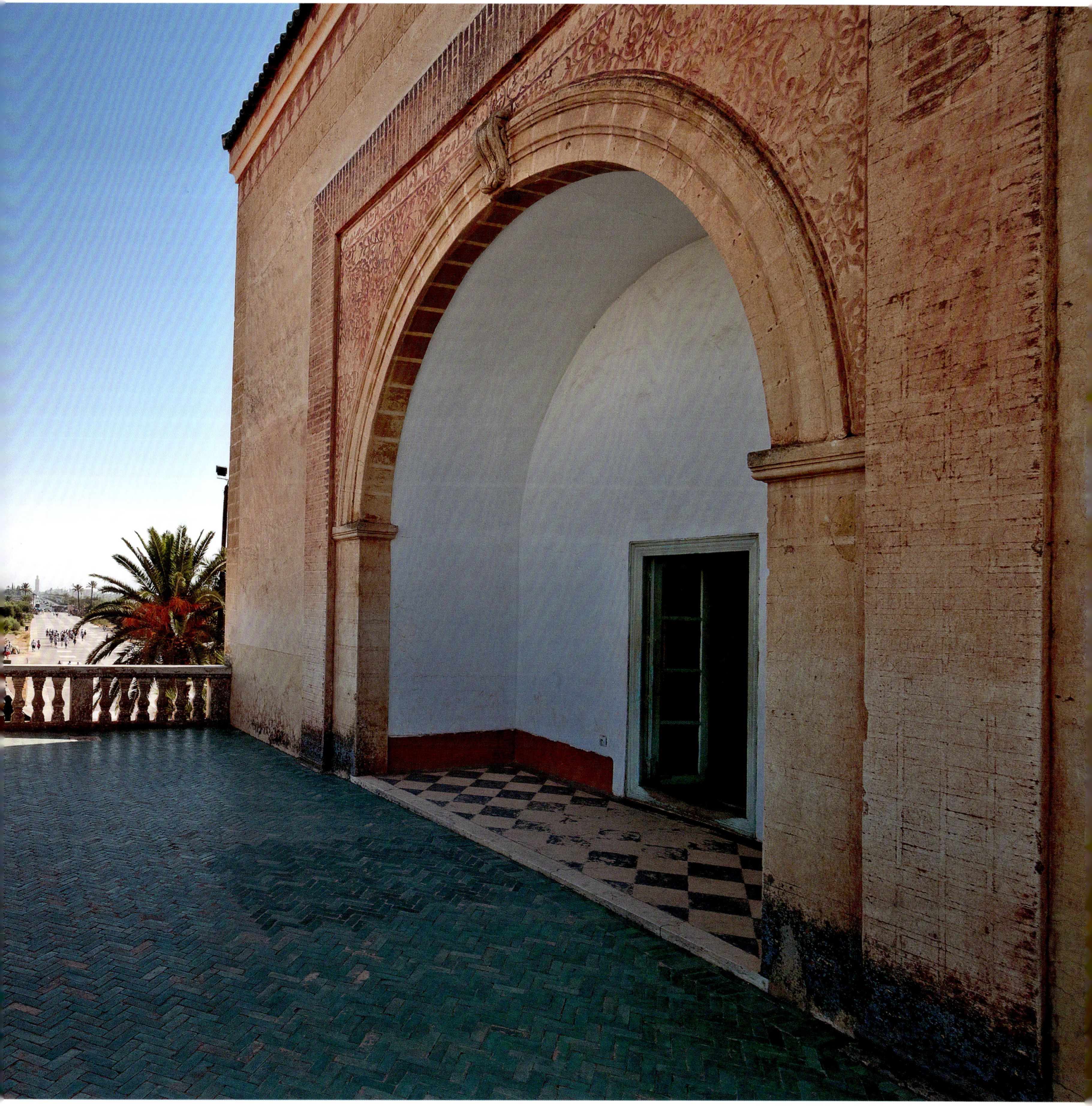

LEFT Views of the Koutoubia minaret dominate the adjacent, French-style Koutoubia Gardens, where bitter orange trees are clipped to form thick discs with brightly coloured roses reaching up to tickle their undersides.

BELOW A small *sahrij* or irrigation basin is set on a mound overlooking a whimsical topiary zigzag hedge of evergreen *Duranta repens*.

RIGHT The garden is full of formal European-style features, such as this avenue of 'Bigaradier Apepu', a much prized variety of bitter orange (*Citrus aurantium*) introduced to France by returning Crusaders.

3. Gardens of the Koutoubia

There is a planning law applicable to the Medina which stipulates that no building should be taller than a palm tree. It is a good rule which has built-in flexibility while clearly making the point that the old city should retain its original low-level character – except for the skyward reach of the minarets which grace its mosques. The queen of these minarets is unequivocally the beautiful, twelfth-century, square tower which adorns the Koutoubia Mosque; justifiably the most famous landmark in the city. Every Friday, between prayers, people crowd into the surrounding gardens, either for a moment of spiritual contemplation or just to be sociable.

The Koutoubia Mosque was built twice. It is thought that the first version, erected in 1147, was discovered to be incorrectly positioned in relation to Mecca, so the very busy Abd el Moumen, who was creating the Agdal and Menara gardens around the same time, started again in 1154. However, since the two mosques coexisted for at least thirty years (and the position of the second mosque is also incorrect), it is possible that it was just too small. Koutoubia means 'mosque of the booksellers' after the manuscript salesmen, or *koutoubeen*, who sold their wares on the site. El Moumen's dynasty subscribed to an ascetic version of Islam which produced a much more sober architecture, with an emphasis on simplicity. Literacy and scholarship were also prized, so dedicating his mosque to these men made the point that he was an educated and godly ruler.

Unfortunately, only Muslims are allowed inside this beautiful building, which contains a courtyard garden whose simple design combines the inward-looking *riad* aesthetic with that of the orchard pleasure garden. Like the *riad* garden, the courtyard is enclosed on all sides and paved, with a central water basin and fountain. However, the typically four-part design multiplies here into twenty-four sections set in a grid pattern, each planted with an orange tree in a sunken well. The result looks very modern and could be part of a new urban piazza, but is a good example of the particularly pared down, simple style, which, combined with quality materials and workmanship, is the hallmark of the Moroccan-Andalusian style of the period.

The Almohads were keen to destroy all vestiges of the previous dynasty, so it is not surprising that Abd el Moumen built his mosque on the site of an Almoravid fortress, the Dar el Hujar, constructed around 1106–42. An archaeological investigation in 1952 discovered a four-part, cross axial garden belonging to this Almoravid stronghold, making it the oldest such garden in Morocco and one of the oldest in the whole Arab world. The simple rectangular courtyard, 45m x 24m, was traversed by water channels, probably supplied by the two cisterns of the present-day mosque courtyard. The resulting four sections would have been planted with vegetation, although exactly what is not known. Today, this piece of garden history is buried again, however, glass-roofed wells near the eastern entrance display vestiges of the original Almoravid building, with the foundations of the first Koutoubia mosque around the corner on the north side. The east forecourt also contains the seventeenth-century tomb of Lalla Zohra, a former slave who is thought to have transformed herself into a dove at night to perform miracles. She continues to have a strong following of mostly female adherents and any baby dedicated to her is forbidden ever to eat pigeon in exchange for her benediction. The very heavy use of the east entrance, the archaeology and the human traffic around the saint's tomb meant that the restoration of the area in 2002 was kept very simple and is mainly paved.

The Islamic-style garden to the south side, however, is potentially an interesting space, with its tall palms, central water basin, orange trees and scented shrubs. Unfortunately at the moment it seems that it is suffering from over use and the effects of pollution from the proximity of a very busy road. Trees are clearly stressed and damaged, the fountain lacks water and litter is an issue. Hopefully these problems will be addressed in the near future so the garden can function as it should, providing a cool and shady place for

28 Gardens of Marrakesh

LEFT AND FAR LEFT The south side of the Koutoubia Mosque is graced with a mainly paved garden with sunken wells providing planting areas for citrus trees, palms and flowering shrubs. Maintenance seems to be a bit of an issue here but as evening falls and the lights of the minaret cast a romantic glow the garden comes into its own.

BELOW The Art Deco fountain and canal in the Koutoubia Gardens give a fascinating glimpse of the desire to marry the latest European style to local Islamic idioms. It would be wonderful see the complex play of jets and sprays as it was intended, but the technology is currently very expensive.

worshippers to gather and rest and a natural screen for the mosque from the temporal world beyond. Meanwhile, the adjacent European-style pleasure gardens, universally known as the Koutoubia Gardens, are green, scented and well kept, attracting a diverse public.

The Koutoubia Gardens were renamed the Park Princess Lalla Hasna in June 2002 after the king's sister who has dedicated her working life to environmental issues. However, such is the powerful presence of the mosque that few people have noted the change, with even recent guidebooks still referring to it by its old name. It is a typical old-fashioned French-style park, made for strolling couples, families and old people taking the air. The pleasant, wide paths are lined with comfortable benches, swathes of colourful roses fill beds defined by strict topiary edging and an avenue of orange trees has been trimmed to form thick discs hung with golden orbs. One of the main built features is clearly a nod to Moroccan-Andalusian culture: a long, colourfully tiled canal, with water sprays, forms part of the main axis of the design which is centred on the Koutoubia minaret. There is also an awkward-looking round pool on this axis and a couple more off to one side which fall between two cultures, looking a bit unresolved. This might be easier to forgive if the water features featured more water, but this seems to be a common problem throughout the Medina. Overall the park has old-world charm, the best framed views of the Koutoubia and very respectable public facilities.

The gardens around the Koutoubia work very hard and as a result are often not as pleasing as they could be. However, there is a moment in the evening when harsher realities can be overlooked. As the sun bleeds the sky orange, and the lights of the minaret switch on, there is a magic in the star-burst silhouettes of palm trees set against the ancient building, and one can imagine Marrakesh the oasis and the wonder it must have been.

Gardens of the Koutoubia

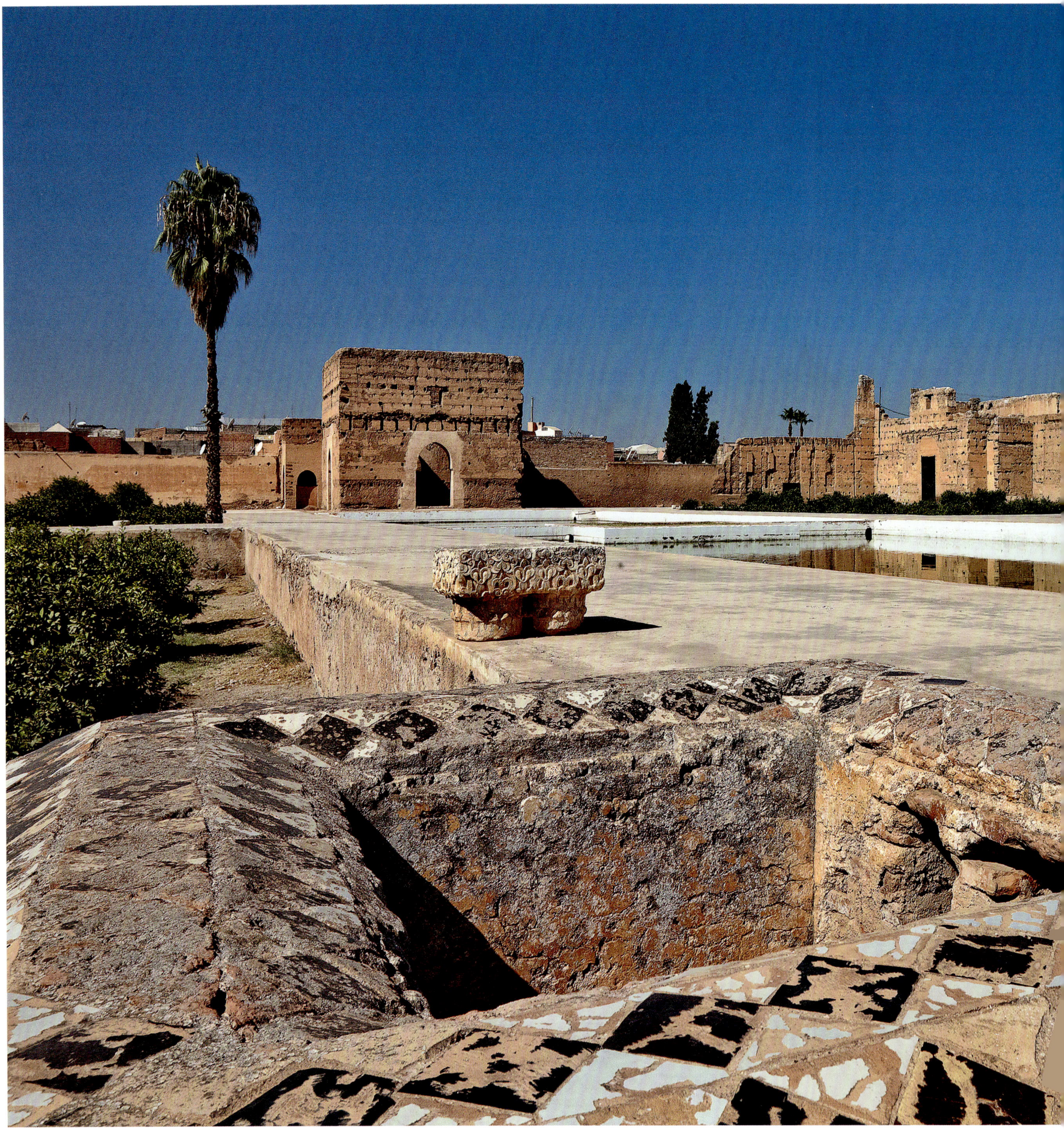

4. The Badi Palace

LEFT The magnificent *riad* courtyard of the Badi Palace was built in 1579 by Sultan Ahmed el Mansour. The ruins today show just the bare bones of what was once a courtyard garden of unimaginable opulence with every surface covered in gold, marble, and intricate *zellij* work, with enamel terracotta tiles used in a multitude of geometric patterns and colour combinations.

The Place Ferblantiers is a lively little square in the south-east of the Medina, denoted by a huge eucalyptus tree and the sound of metal being worked into decorative lanterns. Pass through the archway known as the Bab Berrima and the atmosphere changes instantly. Ahead, hidden from view behind monumental walls and shrouded in a reverent silence, lie the ruins of the once fabled luxury of the Badi Palace, home of Sultan Ahmed el Mansour – El Dahbi (The Golden, r.1578–1603). Visitors today are often not prepared for the impact of this site, which is simultaneously awe-inspiring and unsettling, a monument to human achievement and to its ultimate fragility.

The history of Marrakesh has been marked by the ebb and flow of power between dynasties which variously chose it as their capital or abandoned it for another. The most successful dynasties were able to embellish the city because they provided both political stability and great wealth. Of these the Saadians (1517–1659) stand out as master builders, responsible for achievements such as the Mellah, or Jewish Quarter, as well as many fine mosques and monuments. A cultivated sensibility did not preclude them from being ruthlessly ambitious, with family members challenging each other for power. On 4 August 1578 the very lucky Ahmed el Mansour had it fall into his lap after the Battle of the Three Kings in which the sultan, his nephew the challenger and the nephew's supporter, the King of Portugal, were all killed. El Mansour was an intelligent and erudite ruler who knew the value of myth-making. Five months after his accession to the throne work began on a vast palace which was to be the centre of his court, a place of marvels and a fitting monument to his greatness. The centrepiece of this architectural sensation was to be an immense courtyard garden which would enchant ambassadors and confirm the sultan's position as a force to be reckoned with on the international stage. The initial finance came from enormous ransoms paid by the Portuguese, but later the success of daring wars in the Sudan gave El Mansour control over hugely lucrative trade routes through the Sahara dealing in gold, slaves and sugar. Money was no object and he spent it generously.

El Badi means 'The Incomparable' and is one of the ninety-nine names given to Allah. In associating himself with God's greatness El Mansour was performing a bit of sixteenth-century spin. However, the palace was so large and so expensively decorated that it lived up to its name. The siting also reinforced the new project's pretensions as it redeveloped an Almohad garden attached to the palace of Yacoub el Mansour (r.1184–99) and its mighty *agdal*. It is not known who was responsible for its design but it is generally agreed that it is clearly Andalusian in character and must have been conceived by an architect from Granada.

At the heart of the design is a great ceremonial courtyard of near perfect symmetry, decorated with pools, pavilions and sunken gardens. Overall, the rectangular space measures 153m x 110m and has a large central basin of 90m x 20m, flanked to north and south by four areas of cultivation, sunk 2.5m below ground level. Two projecting pavilions face each other in line with the central basin; the Crystal Pavilion on the east wall and the Pavilion of the Fifty on the west, both of which have a smaller basin on either side of them. These pavilions are almost exact copies of those in the Courtyard of the Lions in the Alhambra and the rectangular proportion of the basin has a precedent in the Courtyard of the Myrtles. While most scholars agree that this plan represents the pinnacle of *riad* design (that is, a building centred around a rectangular, interior, courtyard garden, designed on a quadripartite grid with fountains, fruit trees and aromatic plants), there is something monumental here which is reminiscent of the basins and squares of cultivation of the nearby Agdal.

El Mansour contracted highly skilled artisans from all over Morocco and Europe, making this a truly international project. Records note that he paid them well and even concerned himself with the well-being of their children, freeing them of any worries which would detract from their work. Engineers worked out complicated plans to harness water to spectacular effect, including a sort of central heating/cooling system using copper pipes. They built the courtyard on vaulted brick piers so the pools could be filled to the brim using gravity but could still be level with the principal paths. A spectacular double-bowled fountain placed on a small, square central island, accessed by two narrow causeways, gushed water in the middle of the main pool. All service areas were lodged out of sight underground but mechanical dumb waiters helped move food from the kitchens to the royal family. Materials were transported from around the world and the French writer Montaigne noted that he saw craftsmen near Pisa cutting fifty very tall marble columns for the King of Barbary, which were paid for pound for pound in valuable sugar. What appear today as bare surfaces were all covered in

RIGHT This regal space was designed to be impressive from all angles. From above the five blue pools, four green planted gardens, a central double cupped fountain and sparkling tiled pathways would have resembled the pattern on an intricate carpet.

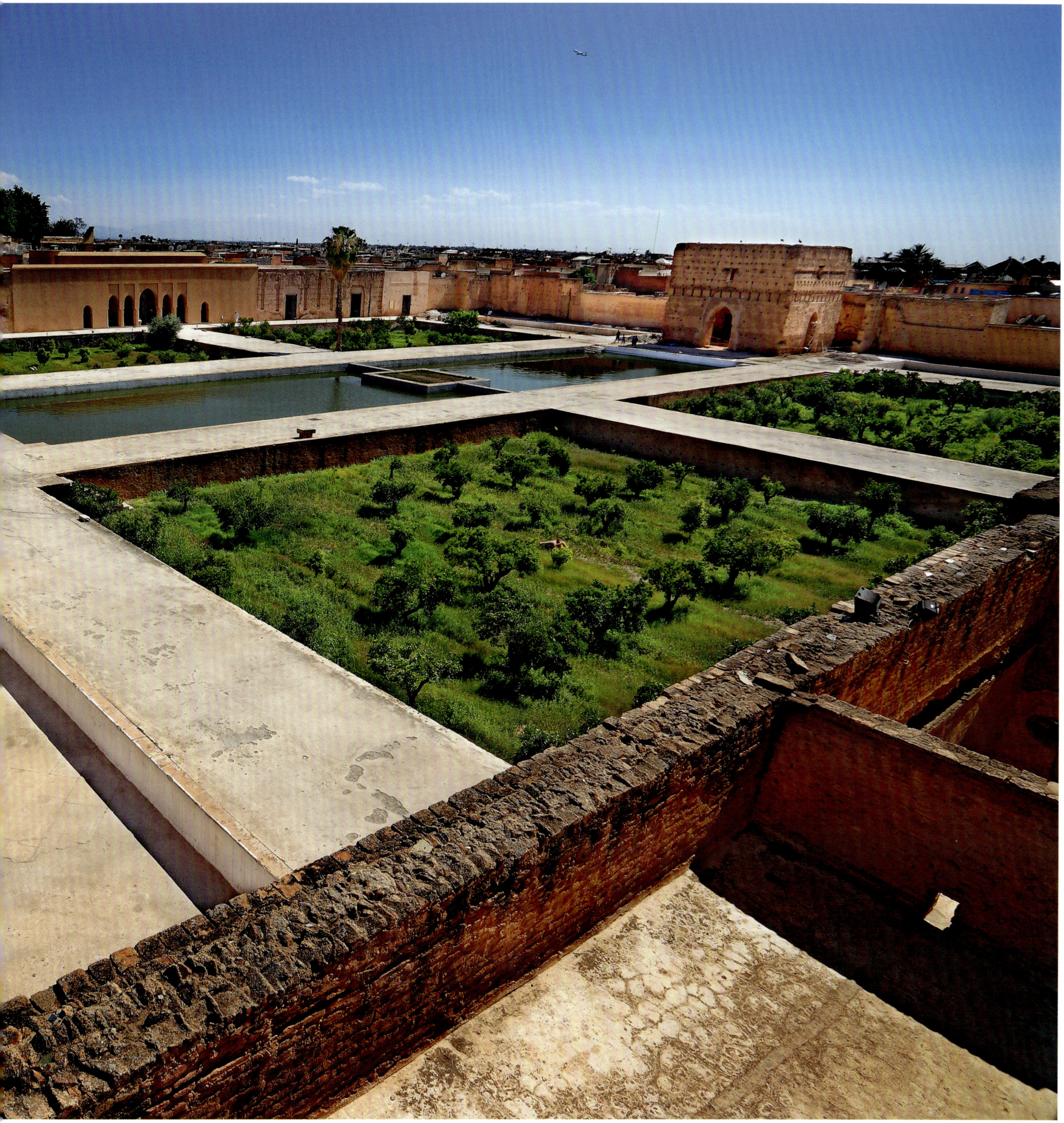

BELOW The Badi was built on brick piers with sophisticated technology allowing for underfloor heating, discrete underground kitchens with hydraulic service lifts and a garden irrigation system using gravity. The sunken areas were planted with citrus in quincunx with herbs and scented flowers enjoying the protected microclimate created by the canopy of the evergreen trees.

RIGHT With the massive rammed earth walls of the Badi Palace on the left and the city walls of the Medina to the right, the current entrance is both impressive and unsettling: qualities of which El Mansour would have approved.

ornamentation, from simple slabs of marble in every conceivable colour, to intricate *zellij*-work pathways and pavilions dressed in gold, onyx, ivory, lapis lazuli and other precious materials.

It is hard to look at the ruins of this architectural marvel and imagine its glorious past. Fortunately there exist several contemporary descriptions and two detailed sketches which flesh out the bones which are left. One of these is an isometric plan which shows that, unlike today, visitors would have entered the palace from the south-east, making their way through a series of gardens until they were invited into the most magnificent of them all. A garden was clearly thought of as being the ultimate in luxury, with sheets of still water a mirror to the sky and playing fountains refreshing the air. The four large sunken planted areas were each gardens in themselves, reached by decorated stairways. Digging gardens below ground level had been a feature of Andalusian design for centuries, with some descending as much as 4.7 metres. The advantage of this system was practical: the gardens were sheltered from the elements, especially from harsh drying winds, and created their own microclimate when planted with evergreen citrus trees, whose canopy created something of a greenhouse effect. They could also be easily watered using a gravity-fed flooding mechanism and provided pockets of privacy in a very busy household. Records suggest that these gardens were filled with Seville oranges, lemons and other citrus trees planted in quincunx with myrtle, jasmine and a variety of scented shrubs and flowers, and aromatic herbs, planted in decorative order between them. The tops of the trees would have been level with that of the pools giving the impression from above of a living carpet. Both pavilions had special viewing rooms above the main salons where visitors would have admired both the perfection of the man-made garden and of the natural grandeur of the snow-capped Atlas Mountains on the horizon.

El Mansour inaugurated his palace in 1593/4 with a magnificent feast to which all the great and good of the land were invited as well as foreign ambassadors. His generosity on this occasion towards both his guests and people was unprecedented. However, it is said that when El Mansour asked his clairvoyant what he thought of his wonderful palace he replied, 'Sire, when this is all in ruins it will make a huge pile of stones'. In Islamic numerology the Badi's name is equivalent to the inauspicious number 117. This is exactly the number of lunar years the opulent palace survived before a new sultan from a new dynasty dismantled it and recycled its treasures in Meknes, his chosen capital.

36 Gardens of Marrakesh

5. The Bahia Palace

The complex of buildings and gardens which make up the Bahia Palace has been described by the scholar Mohammed El Faïz as 'the last showcase built to the glory of the architecture and art of garden making of Marrakesh'. This beautiful and sophisticated place has, in the past, also been called shoddy, vulgar and ill conceived – the work of a degenerate, late nineteenth-century nouveau-riche family, seeking self-aggrandisement. The gap in perception arose from a cultural divide which left most westerners bewildered and without any useful reference point. To some extent this is still the case. Visitors from the European tradition expect their palace architecture to be monumental, with plenty of gilding and glitter surrounded by extensive and masterful gardens. The Bahia offers a different vision of wealth and power, in which the relationship between architecture, gardens and felicitous, communal family living in a desert context is paramount.

The Bahia Palace is in the south of the city, just a stone's throw from the Badi Palace, but the two sites, which both celebrate great personal success, show very different faces to the world. The huge walls of the Badi shout omnipotence and, rather like the great Almohad gardens of the Menara and Agdal, the visitor gets the message in one powerful hit. The Bahia by contrast is experienced as a visual and emotional journey with barely a whisper of glory at the gate. The reason for this is largely pragmatic. In 1894 when Ahmed ben Moussa, known as Bahmad, decided to create a palace to rival the Badi he chose a property he had inherited from his father, the Riad Si Moussa, as his starting point. Bahmad came from a family whose members had made their name working as high level civil servants to the court of the Alaouite sultans. On the death of his father in 1878 Bahmad had inherited a considerable fortune which enabled him to enlarge his chosen site by the speedy and expensive purchase of sixty buildings and sixteen private gardens. His next problem was how to rationalise these various plots into a palace of more than three hectares with an *agdal* of 19.5 hectares, all in a record time of five to six years. He delegated this problem to the renowned local architect Haj Mohammed ben el-Mekki el-Mesfioui. El-Mesfioui had trained in the School of Moroccan Architecture which taught its students both the value of working with existing structures and the importance of integrating nature into their projects. His genius was in being able to compose a masterly design from a patchwork of disparate elements.

Today the Bahia Palace is occasionally used by the royal family to house guests and is the home of the Moroccan Ministry of Cultural Affairs. It is also a major tourist attraction where visitors are offered a condensed tour of some of the best the palace has to offer including three important courtyard gardens. The first of these, and the youngest, is that of the Petit Riad (Riad es-Sghir), completed in 1898, just two years before the death of Bahmad. As is typical of *riad* architecture the garden comes as a surprise after a series of changing levels, blank walls and zigzagging corridors. What increases the impact of this delicious little courtyard is the simplicity of the decoration in the building before you burst into a richly adorned quadripartite garden with glowing, multi-coloured tile work, fabulously intricate plasterwork and carved cedar panels. The four planted areas are surrounded with a balustrade, which was typical of the period and was filled mainly with Seville oranges, bananas and a froth of dark green ground cover. Light streams in, filtered through the boughs of the tall trees hung with oranges, and birds in flight create moments of drama as their shadows pass overhead. This refined and sophisticated space, with its central marble basin, seating niche and porticoes, was used as a reception room for guests and a place where verses of the Koran were recited.

On leaving the Petit Riad you pass into the heart of the palace proper. Filing through various richly decorated salons, simply tiled courtyards and theatrically dark corridors, you exit suddenly into the sunlight of the famous Marble Courtyard. It is said that the palace gets its name from the reaction of visitors who, on seeing this space, cried out '*bahiya! bahiya!*' (beautiful, brilliant). Constructed in 1896–97 the plantless courtyard measures 30m x 50m and is divided into quadrants by paths of multi-coloured *zellij* in a simple chequered pattern. Each quadrant is paved in white marble (possibly originally from the Badi Palace), with borders of *zellij* around each large slab. These warm throughout the day and radiate a gentle heat in the evening making for a very pleasant barefooted stroll. The large rectangular central fountain with its two attendant round basins would have animated the space with the sound of running water and the surrounding open air galleries, supported on delicate fluted wooden pillars, would have provided shade from the midday sun. The purity of the balance achieved in the composition suggests that there was more intended here than just a grand effect. Could it have

FAR LEFT The Marble Courtyard is said to have been such a fabulous sight that visitors cried out '*bahiya! bahiya!*' (beautiful, brilliant) in admiration, thus giving the palace its popular name. The current restoration programme is aiming for the same kind of reaction when work on the exquisite woodwork, paving, fountains and painted panels is completed in 2014.

LEFT This simple, whitewashed, patio courtyard has recently been restored to its former pristine condition.

The Bahia Palace 37

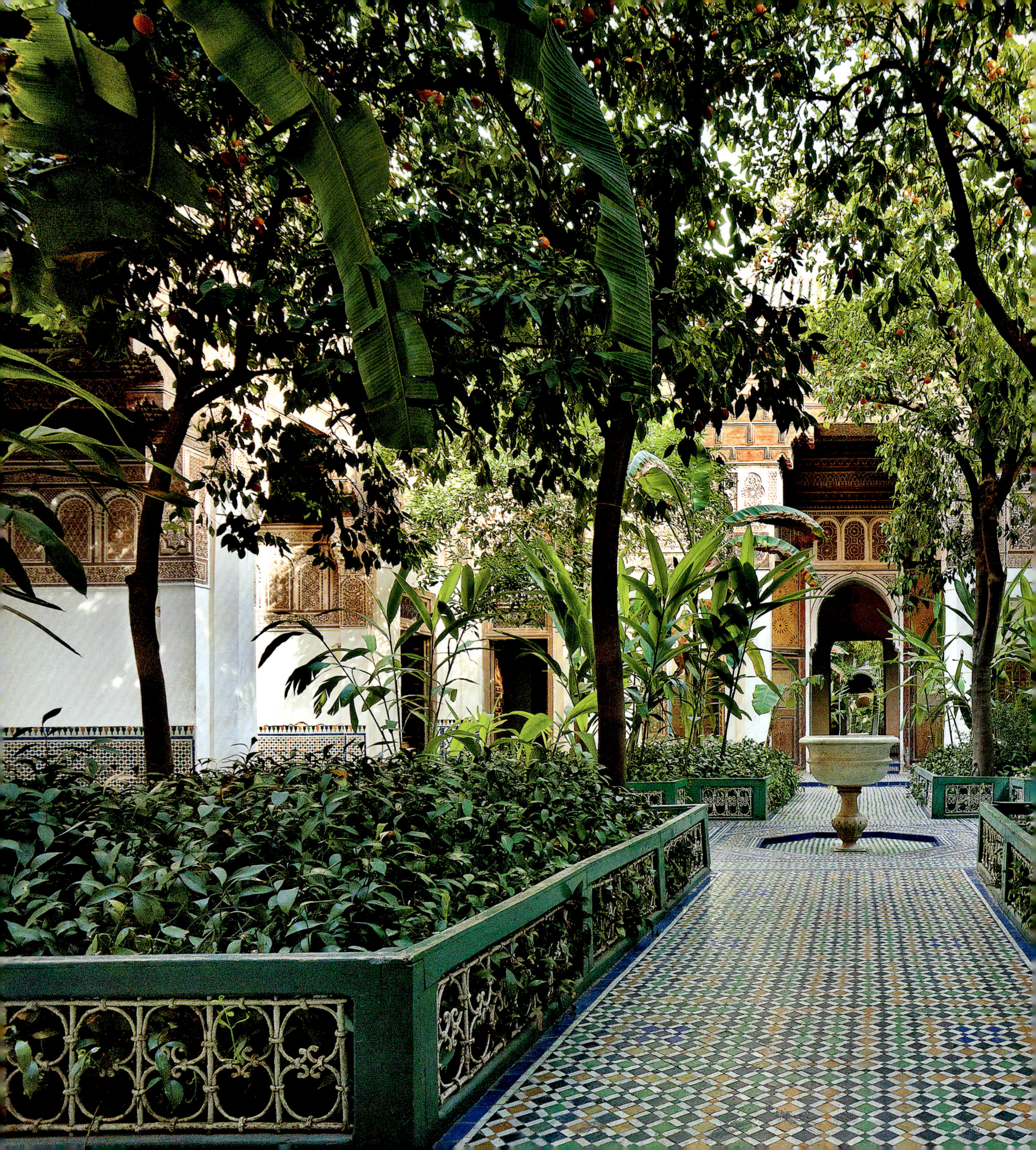

LEFT The Petit Riad of the Bahia Palace gives a master class in proportion and balance. The four planted areas contain orange trees, underplanted with a bubbling froth of Horse Tongue Lily, *Ruscus hypoglossum*, a drought-resistant and shade-loving perennial, possibly used to make the laurel wreaths of Caesars.

ABOVE It is not always possible or practical to have real plants in the domestic spaces of the palace but painted plants and flowers appear everywhere: on doors, shutters and ceilings.

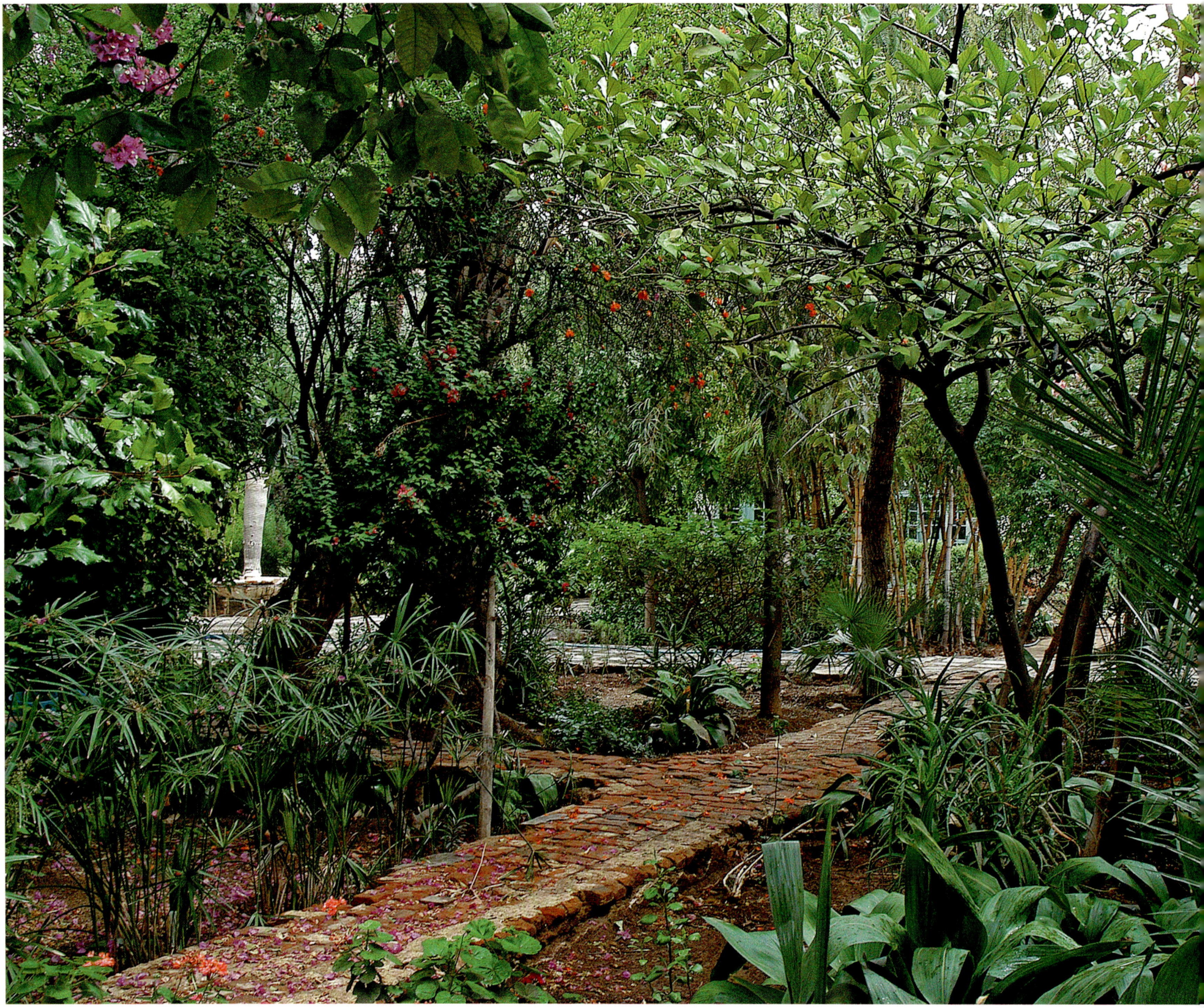

been a desire to capture a piece of the sky in a frame, or to make a mirror for the great cosmos above? Or perhaps it was simply a counterbalance to the adjacent garden beyond.

Passing through a gateway to the side of the Marble Courtyard you step down into a traditional *riad* garden filled with luxuriant plants, sweet perfume and playing fountains. The Grand Riad, or the Riad Si Moussa, was the heart of the old complex built by Sidi Moussa, the father of Bahmad. Built to please his favourite wife, the garden has a unique pastoral charm, despite adhering strictly to the formula for a *riad* garden. Its rectangular form, entirely enclosed, with delightful garden pavilions at each end, a quadripartite plan and central fountain, comes as no surprise. However the plan is further divided into quadrants with raised paths between each section inviting a wander through the enchantments of a myriad of flowering plants and trees, herbs and scented climbers, citrus fruit and peaches. There are marble fountains aligned down the central axis which must have refreshed the air, and caged birds were used to lure wild ones to animate the scene. This was a garden of perfection where every desire was satisfied except perhaps the longing for space and a distant horizon.

From beyond the far end of the Marble Courtyard there appear the tops of tall cypress and palm trees. These belong to another rectangular garden with a superb central basin and the remains of a complex hydraulic system, all of which have been abandoned to nature. Bahmad was mad about gardens and would have been familiar with the history of the great ones of the region. In contrast to those designed in the spirit of outdoor rooms he wanted to adorn his palace (and thereby his reputation as a powerful and civilised man) with gardens on a large scale. This 'lost' space appears to have been designed to look like an *agdal* in miniature, announcing the real one which was reached by an enclosed bridge spanning the road which separated it from the palace buildings. Here he developed an enormous 19.5 hectare, trapezoid site into one of the wonders of the era, based on the features of the Royal Agdal, with a wonderful view of the Atlas Mountains, but on a reduced scale. Only a fragment of the Agdal Bahmad exists today but the great irrigation basin is being restored and there are those who are fighting to keep what is left as part of the heritage of the Bahia. Canny Bahmad realised the value of a productive garden so close to the markets of the Medina and it is interesting to note that he grew high value crops which he could sell at a premium, exploiting the attraction of local produce. In fact the 1952 edition of the French Guide Bleu remarks on the thrice-weekly markets, held during the months of December to February, where Bahmad's oranges and mandarins could be bought '*fraîchement cueillies*', just picked. This idea is very much in tune with modern ideals of the urban farm movement and perhaps Bahmad's garden could once more supply the city with fresh food.

Bahmad and his palace have taken a fair bit of abuse in the past. Colonial writers wrongly interpreted the ground plan as a warren, built by an evil vizier, to better evade constant attempts on his life. Even the elegance of single-storey *riad* architecture was interpreted as a response to his weak knees. Fortunately both Bahmad's reputation and the Bahia are being restored and the gardens of the Grand Riad and Marble Courtyard, currently closed, are due to reopen with a new lease of life at the end of 2013.

LEFT The Bahia Palace's magical Riad Si Moussa was created at some time between 1859 and 1873, by Bahmad's father for his favourite wife. An unruly assortment of plants, including pelargoniums, bougainvillea, abutilon, palms and papyrus sedge, is allowed freedom of expression within a formal setting, like a bouquet of wild flowers in a vase.

ABOVE The central axis is marked by a marble fountain, with the yellow and green stems of *Bambusa vulgaris* 'Vittata' (painted bamboo) making a striking feature to the left of the picture.

BELOW A paved, central courtyard garden, without plants, is known as an *ouest ed-dar*, or patio. Surfaces are decorated with multi-coloured *zellij* tiles which often imitate the effect of real blooms and are designed to reflect light and to scintillate. An elaborate wall fountain, or *seqqaya*, and central marble *khossa*, a cup-shaped fountain, animate the space with the sound of life-giving water and keep the courtyard cool.

6. Dar Si Said

It is just a ten minute leisurely stroll from the Bahia Palace to the Dar Si Said which houses the Museum of Moroccan Arts; but whereas the former is usually crammed with tourists the latter is often overlooked so, if you are lucky, it can be blissfully empty. The collection itself may not have the wow factor but beyond its whitewashed, vaulted corridors and stark ground floor apartments, the mansion contains a well-guarded secret – a garden of chocolate box perfection.

The Dar Si Said is in many ways a concentrated version of the Bahia Palace, built concurrently using the same artisans by Bahmad's brother, Si Said ben Moussa. Family ties are strong in Morocco but before the second half of the nineteenth century the political structures of the state ensured that individual families could not easily build up vast personal wealth. The weakening of central state control after 1850 allowed such fortunes to be made in trade, taxation and property. As will be seen in the entries on the Riad Mounia, Enija and Madani, many of the men who made money in this period spent it on palatial architecture and gardens, collectively financing a renaissance of the arts in Marrakesh. In 1894 Bahmad effectively controlled Morocco as Grand Vizier with plenipotentiary powers to Sultan Moulay Abd al-Aziz (r.1894–1908), who was still a minor. He made his brother, Si Said, Minister of War, so it was convenient for them to live in close proximity and only fitting that Si Said should also have a prestigious new home.

A *dar* is essentially a very large house built on more than one storey with several interior courtyards, some finely decorated and others more utilitarian. Si Said's mansion has a positively urban feel as it appears to fit seamlessly into the dense architecture of the winding *derbs,* showing only its massive wooden entrance door to the passing public. Inside there are three principal outdoor spaces: a roof terrace which has wonderful views over the whole city and of the Atlas Mountains, a fine tiled courtyard and a delightful *riad* garden. Unfortunately the roof is off-limits to the public and, at the time of writing, there is restricted access to the tiled courtyard too, though it is possible to view it from an upper chamber from where the star-shaped *zellij* centrepiece is best admired. Such tiled courtyards are often referred to as *patios* and are typical of *dar* architecture where limited space and high walls meant that it was more practical to decorate them with colourful *zellij* than to fill them with plants. Tiles also had the advantage of being cool in the heat of the summer (bearing in mind that much of life was spent at ground level), easy to keep clean, and allowing flexibility in the arrangement of the luxurious soft furnishings of the household. However practical and pretty, this is little more than a room open to the sky with none of the pleasure a living garden brings – for that you have to negotiate a somewhat tortuous corridor which ends in a patch of daylight through a doorway.

It has been observed that although Si Said was intellectually far less able than his brother Bahmad he had more time and better taste to devote to the creation of his home. That is a debatable view, but stepping into the perfumed elegance of his lush *riad* garden filled with an array of citrus trees, flowering shrubs and aromatic herbs, it is easy to see why he might have gained such a reputation. Although the whole ensemble is known as a *dar*, this part of the house takes the form of a *riad*. It is on one floor with the garden being a perfectly proportioned rectangle with beautiful triple arcaded loggias at either end. The paths which define the four-part design are tiled in a zigzag pattern of glazed green and cream oblong tiles whose soft gleam magnifies the optical illusion of running water – the four rivers of Paradise described in the Koran. The central fountain is contained in a tiled octagonal basin and protected by a graceful wooden kiosk supported by eight columns. The ceiling of this structure is painted with delicate floral motifs which must have looked wonderful when bright and fresh but which have faded over time. The roof too would have been strikingly dressed with *quermoud*, the green-glazed tiles which can be seen fringing the courtyard. These clay tiles, enamelled with copper oxide are expensive and were used exclusively on mosques, palaces and prestigious buildings. The striking decoration of the paths, loggias and kiosk is mainly achieved in four colours, red, yellow, green and blue with the surrounding whitewashed walls brightening the effect. To the uninitiated these colours are attractive but to the educated Muslim they are meaningful and add to the experience of the garden.

Colour in Islam is seen from a metaphysical viewpoint as is mathematics. The intellectual systems built around a combination of the two can be mind-bogglingly complex but the number 7 dominates the traditional palette, made up of 3 plus 4. The 3 are: white, which represents the light of the sun and is a manifestation of God's power; black, in which colours remain concealed from their own brightness as God hides his own radiance; and light brown sandalwood, which is thought of as 'colourless earth', the neutral ground on which nature and the polar properties of black and white take effect. The 4 are: red = fire; yellow = air; green = water and blue = earth. Green is also the colour of Islam so it is easy to see how cultural misunderstandings occur; a green-tiled path could easily be thought to represent vegetation but to Si Said it would have been an obvious reference to water, the heavenly gift of the creator.

In a troubled time the Minister for War must have found welcome respite from his duties in this garden where water and fruit, cool

44 Gardens of Marrakesh

shade, perfumed plants and a calming geometry would have eased his mind. However he had just a few years to contemplate the cypress trees he planted here as a symbol of mortality. In 1900 both Si Said and his brother Bahmad died within hours of each other, possibly poisoned victims of a political conspiracy. Their homes were immediately ransacked of valuables and their families dispersed. The beautiful *riad* garden survives as Si Said's legacy.

LEFT AND ABOVE In contrast to the reality of the bustling world outside, the *riad* garden at Dar Si Said is a haven of peace and harmony, a veritable poem to the senses. Beautiful green and white glazed tiles imitate the ripple of water and are cool and smooth underfoot. The central fountain is protected by a kiosk, decorated with hand-painted blooms in jewel box colours. Small songbirds are busy among the trees and no sound from the outside world disturbs the atmosphere of retreat. Most striking of all is the perfume of *Brugmansia arborea*, whose white blooms release such a heavenly scent that their common name, Angel's Trumpet, seems doubly apt.

BELOW The Jardin Bouachrine is all that remains of the Grand Vizier's *arsat*. Tall and stately olive trees, a little battered and bruised but still standing, are a reminder that this area is known as Zitoun – meaning olive.

7. Riad Mounia

It was with a certain sense of trepidation that Maryvonne and Alain Grunberg broke the police seal on the door of the mystery property they had inherited. Standing in the derelict *riad* garden, surrounded by collapsing walls and a gaggle of curious local children, they knew that accepting this legacy would turn their lives upside down. However it was a challenge that the two history teachers from Tours could not resist; they were clearly fated to save this beautiful, nineteenth-century architectural gem from destruction.

Situated near the Bahia Palace, in the area locals call the Palace or Andalusian Quarter, the Riad Mounia was built in 1860 at the start of an extraordinary building boom which has been discussed in the previous entry on the Dar Si Said. It was part of a palace complex consisting of three interconnecting *riads* and several small *dars*, built by Grand Vizier Bouachrine, Prime Minister to Sultan Sidi Mohammed (r.1859–73). The current Riad Mounia was his reception hall for visiting male supplicants and honoured guests and had four main rooms with a traditional central courtyard garden, all splendidly adorned to impress. Documents show that visitors entered the complex via the adjacent *arsat* planted with olive trees, part of which survives as a public garden – the Jardin Bouachrine. The desire to own an *arsat* in this period shows that they were considered a status symbol, a must-have for any successful man, rather as a landscape park was in Europe.

Bouachrine broke with the norm in Marrakesh, where a *riad* was strictly a ground-hugging structure, and built on more than one storey in the style of hilly Fes, where a shortage of suitable building sites led to houses growing upwards. Maryvonne believes that he started a fashion which was copied in buildings such as the later phase of the Bahia Palace and the Dar Si Said. Artisans from Fes were also imported for the interiors where they showed off their skill in lusciously painted woodwork, glowing mosaics and carved plaster. Bouachrine would have received visitors in these chambers, wandering from room to room doing business in the traditional spoken fashion, with the men refreshing themselves in the cool of the garden. In fact the garden here is cooler than most as the extra storey has the negative effect of reducing sunlight and air, making the gardener's job a little more difficult.

Homes in the Medina are about privacy and the sanctity of family life and as we have seen this is reflected in many aspects of *riad* architecture. The outside world is firmly excluded, so today all that is visible of the Riad Mounia from the street is a simple wooden door and blank walls. Once inside the visitor passes along a zigzag of passages which shield the inner sanctum from prying eyes to emerge into the light and delight of the garden – the emotional and physical heart of the house. Maryvonne knew that the design of the garden was crucial to the overall integrity of her restoration, but while the quadripartite form was apparent, the tiled pathways were beyond repair, the water basin and fountain smashed and most of the plants dead. Fortunately she came across help in the form of an interesting book, written in 1926 by Jean Gallotti, *Le Jardin et la Maison Arabes au Maroc*, which is full of intelligent description and sketches of the Moroccan tradition. Apart from providing excellent source material, Gallotti evokes the spirit of the *riad* garden describing it as, 'a little bit of nature gathered from beyond the city, like a bouquet, and placed in a vase in the middle of the house'.

Maryvonne's garden reflects Gallotti's observations and adheres in spirit to the basic blueprint for all *riad* garden design, but it is an interpretation rather than a strict recreation. The paths which define the four-part structure have been tiled in small terracotta bricks which remind her of her native Normandy, interspaced with a scintillating pattern of green and blue *zellij* tiles. Originally these paths would probably have been paved with marble from Carrara, divided by decorative bands of coloured mosaic, but the cost of this was prohibitive. Instead Maryvonne chose a pattern she found during her research at the Institute for Arab Studies in Paris relating to a *medersa* in Bokhara on the Silk Route. She has continued the colour scheme through to the decoration of the wall fountain and the octagonal *sahrij*, or basin, centrally placed at the node of the two axial paths. A *khossa*, cup-shaped fountain, rises from its coloured base in pure white contrast. Maryvonne fills it with cut flowers, as if it were literally a vase. The elements which make up the structure of the garden are used to connect the outside space with the interiors. This is just an outside room, open to the sky, decorated by nature. The formality of the design, where feet are never intended to step on soil, contrasts strongly with an informal approach to the plants themselves.

The Grunbergs have subscribed to the Islamic garden tradition which regards plants as honoured guests and have allowed their plants to express their true nature with little constraint or regulation. All the planting had to be renewed, apart from the date palms and the white mulberry, and they intentionally chose a mixture of traditional species and personal favourites such as the olive. Although olive trees were highly valued they were never included in *riad* planting. However, they have a family significance for the Grunbergs and are also a reminder that the whole district was once an olive grove and still bears the name Zitoun meaning olive.

Many of the plants in the garden have a story to tell but it is perhaps the young fig which has the most unusual. When the

48 Gardens of Marrakesh

Grunbergs first arrived they searched everywhere for the title deeds to the property. On the point of despair Maryvonne remembered that French people used to call their countrymen born in Morocco '*troncs de figuier*' – fig tree trunks. She found what she was looking for wrapped up in a rusty sardine tin, deep in the rotted trunk of an ancient fig. That fig could not be revived but a young replacement is reaping the benefit of special care from a grateful owner.

FAR LEFT The Riad Mounia is unusual as it has more than one storey, which means it can be enjoyed from this elevated perspective. Although the extra height reduces the amount of light reaching the garden, this is counterbalanced by Maryvonne's choice of blue tiles which seem to add sparkle and movement to the area.

LEFT A *seqqaya*, or wall fountain, is a traditional element in *riad* architecture but this one has real personality with a modern twist.

BELOW A turquoise painted table displays old Moroccan pottery and metal objects. The marble fountain behind is decorated with roses but instead of the more usual rose petals, Maryvonne chooses to stand whole stems in the water, using the fountain as a vase.

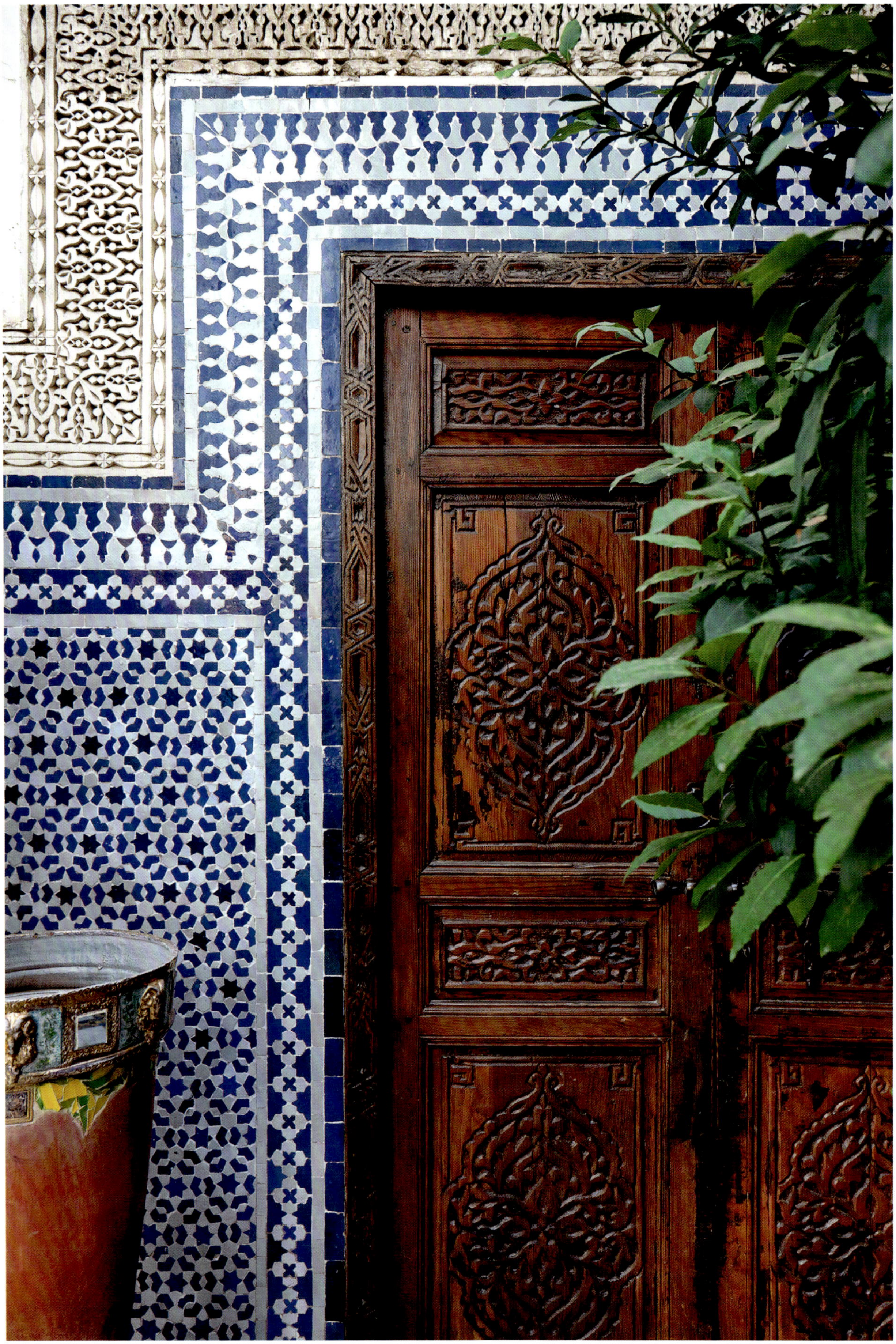

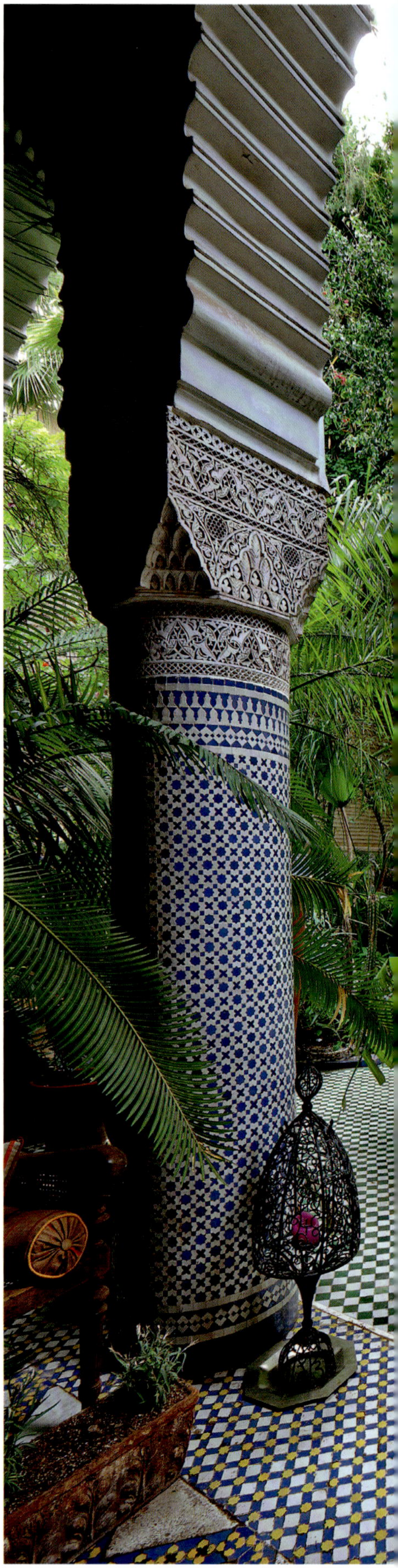

8. Riad Enija

FAR LEFT Blue and white is a very popular colour combination for *zellij* tiling, but more typical of Fes than Marrakesh. The walls of the loggia at either end of the *riad* garden are richly decorated with a frieze of delicately incised plasterwork, known as *geps*, defining the area between colourful tiles and plain white wall above.

LEFT Pattern upon pattern, layer upon layer, the complexity of the *riad* garden has been built up with patience and time, a patina which the owners were keen not to destroy.

Getting to the Riad Enija is something of an obstacle course. Situated in the Rahba Kedima quarter, it is in the thick of the souks where traders line the narrow streets and people weave their way through jostling crowds, donkey carts, bicycles and motorbikes overloaded with lethal cargoes. But a parallel world exists behind the simple studded wooden door at the end of the narrow lane that is the Derb Mesfioui.

The Swedish architect Björn Conerdings and his Swiss designer wife Ursula Haldimann viewed more than two hundred properties in the Medina before being seduced by the beauty of the Riad Enija in the late 1990s. The original building was constructed in the 1730s by a local dignitary as a collection of seven interconnected *dars* with a *riad* garden at its heart. But the building we see today is the legacy of a wealthy silk merchant from Fes who bought the complex in 1860 to accommodate his forty-two family members. He simplified the plan to include just four houses, two patio courtyards, the *riad* and linking corridors. Artisans from his home city were commissioned to decorate the surfaces in the more complex taste of Fes. Björn and Ursula were struck by an intrinsic sense of peace achieved by the volumes of the architecture, the gently faded decoration and the large garden of over 1500 square metres. Stepping over the threshold today, one is struck by the easy symbiosis of the traditional architecture and the modern pieces with which Ursula has embellished the house. The common denominator is respect for harmony, equilibrium and a life well lived. These qualities are reflected in the extraordinarily luxuriant garden where nature has been given full rein to express itself within a space of mathematically perfect proportions.

Ursula describes the garden as having been shabby, with three cypresses, some oranges, a palm and a mulberry as the only vestiges of the nineteenth-century planting plan. The basic structure however was largely intact – an elegant rectangular space divided in four with a central basin and grandly porticoed terraces at either end. The couple restored the old tile work with a gentle touch, valuing the patina achieved by years of use, and cajoled the remaining trees into health. However, they do not believe that tradition should be a tyranny, so have not faithfully reproduced a traditional *riad* garden, but rather expressed their vision of nature as a free spirit with the power to affect the human condition profoundly. Ursula believes that gardeners need to allow plants 'the possibility to just live – just be', which in essence exactly reflects Islamic values. She has filled the planting areas with a multitude of different species, combining colours and textures to produce such an intensity of plant life that the garden risks being overwhelming in its exuberance. It is difficult

52 Gardens of Marrakesh

LEFT There are several stunning courtyards at the Enija besides the important *riad* garden. In this tiled patio courtyard potted palms have been used to dramatic, sculptural effect. To the left a pair of *Trachycarpus fortunei* sit squat, like two exotically plumed birds on their nests. The star of the show though is undoubtedly a magnificent *Dypsis decaryi*, or Triangle Palm. A native of the Madagascan rainforest, it is best displayed as here, with a lot of space around its graceful arching fronds.

BELOW Ursula found this 1950s-style armchair in the city's famous flea market at the Bab Khemis. It has been reupholstered using vintage fabric in contrasting stripes and florals and sits very comfortably in the traditional décor of the loggia at Riad Enija.

to negotiate one's way to the two small seating areas through the thick vegetation which spills out over the pathways. The ever-present risk of tripping over a large tortoise or two, making their stately way to an indeterminate destination, adds to the sense of being a bit of a Jungle Jim.

This aesthetic, akin to an enveloping over-stuffed sofa, is only possible because many of the plants are in pots. The roots of the existing trees have occupied most of the allotted space, so terracotta pots of various shapes and sizes have been incorporated into the design to provide new plants with a suitable home. They lend a sculptural element while often echoing the personality of individual species, short and robust, tall and elegant, curvy and voluptuous. The containers also exaggerate the layered dimension of the planting with the canopy of the tall trees creating a microclimate within which various subtropical species thrive, rather like a European hothouse. The interplay of light and shadow on the plants adds further complexity to these layers, as well as a mystical atmosphere. For many Muslims, light is the symbol of divine unity and exploiting the contrast between light and shade is a vital component of their architecture, its ever changing quality a metaphor for life itself.

The exciting lushness of the garden is, however, on the point of tipping into wild abandon, and Ursula admits to the need for judicious pruning. 'We have to intervene at times to give health, but if we cut something, it hurts Björn's heart, so he retires to the kitchen until it is done.' It is said that the presence of birds is a sign of a healthy garden, and if that is so, there is little cause to worry about the Enija – birds are everywhere. Each year in summer the resident species are visited by hundreds of migrants who replenish their batteries in this haven of green, shattering the calm with their excited chatter, but they move on soon enough, and peace and tranquillity is restored to this mystical urban jungle.

RIGHT The loggia at Riad Enija provides a sheltered place from which to sit and enjoy the play of light and shade, the scent of flowers and foliage, the gentle trickle of the fountain and the chatter of a multitude of birds.

FAR RIGHT The *riad* is jungle-like in its density, with pots of different shapes and sizes clustered together, providing the right conditions for individual species. This device allows for greater diversity, considering the difficult conditions, where the lion's share of nutrients goes to the established trees.

Riad Enija 55

56 Gardens of Marrakesh

9. Riad Madani

FAR LEFT Homero loves the simple generosity and glowing little flowers of the plumbago family. Here, *Plumbago auriculata* has been trained over an arch in the *riad* to frame a view of the beautifully painted niche, which makes the perfect hideout on hot afternoons.

LEFT A simple linking passageway is turned into a melodramatic event by the use of a brooding shade of magenta twinned with the green tiled floor. Potted bananas interspersed with young *Philodendron bipinnatifidum* add hot tropical notes.

Finding a private address is not always easy in Marrakesh. Road signs are a relatively new phenomenon and there is no comprehensive map of the city as yet, so directions are given the old fashioned way, relative to known landmarks. There is always some distinguishing feature, but to locate the Riad Madani in the crush of the souks is particularly easy as this *derb* (lane) is notable for its greenery: a bevy of assorted plants in large green-painted tin cans and, overhead, a flourishing *daliya*, or trellis draped with a trained grapevine. There is no name plaque, but that is not a problem, this is Marrakesh and there is always someone around willing to help.

The Riad Madani is one of the most notable in the Medina, both for its size and for its architecture. It is also redolent with history as it was built in the mid nineteenth century for the Grand Vizier Madani el Glaoui, a shrewd politician and fearless warlord from the Berber Glaoui tribe of the High Atlas. Siding with the French, he enriched himself by filling the power vacuum created by the chaotic politics of the era. His younger brother T'hami el Glaoui was to achieve fame and fabulous wealth as Lord of the Atlas, virtually a feudal despot, who kept order with his 77 mm Krupp cannon. There is nothing fierce about the house today, except perhaps the collection of African tribal shields and weaponry belonging to owner Homero Machry.

The *riad* garden is one of the largest in the Medina, but, as usual, it does not show itself to any casual visitor. This is a treat reserved for those who are invited through corridors and antechambers before emerging into the light, verdure and fragrance of the garden. True to type the garden is rectangular in shape, with four paths which divide the space into quadrants, and a basin in the centre. A generous walkway allows for an easy promenade around the blocks of planting which are dense and luxuriant, full of texture and mystery. There is a strange poetry about the somewhat hectic range of trees, shrubs and flowering climbers which seem to have sprung from the ground of their own accord. Clumps of bananas jostle with oranges, olives, jacaranda, fig and palms of several varieties. Clouds of delicate white and blue plumbago are a feminine counterbalance to virile, spiky stands of *Chamaerops humilis*, with monstera, acanthus, geranium, tradescantia, rosemary, bamboo and pots of dwarf pomegranate each contributing to the complexity of texture. Climbing plants, such as nocturnally scented Queen of the Night (*Cestrum nocturnum*) and the gorgeous Pink Trumpet Vine (*Podranea ricasoliana*), drape themselves over any offered support, generous both in their bloom and perfume. This is not a plant palette to please the purist but the feel of nature, free to express itself, is completely authentic.

For many all this exoticism is exciting and new, a lush world of giant leaves and showgirl blooms, but for Homero Machry it is a taste of home. Homero is a Brazilian in his fifties who appears to be everything a stereotypical Brazilian should be: good looking, sun kissed, stylish in an informal way and with a smile which lights up an already sunny garden. Dressed in his signature sarong and polo shirt, his easy manner and ready laugh belie the stress of his working life in Paris as a top PR consultant and party organiser, with high-profile and exigent clients including famous fashion houses. Everything he organises has to be perfect, every time, so it is not surprising that he finds life in Marrakesh a powerful antidote. He bought the rambling house over a decade ago with his friend, French writer and politician, Thierry de Beaucé, as a place to relax and entertain his phalanx of friends. Homero quietly describes himself as a country boy at heart, recalling that he wanted to give the Madani a country house look, that of an established family home in tune with nature.

This was his first garden and his eyes shine as he tells its story. 'It was a dustbowl, there was practically nothing left, I had to start from scratch.' The structure was still in place, though the paths were crumbling, with two centenarian cypress trees making a last stand. Homero thought of redesigning the space to include a swimming pool but made the costly decision to situate the pool on the roof terrace instead in order to save the integrity of the *riad* garden. Despite having no real experience of gardening, expeditions to the local Pepinières Royales nursery bore fruit as he instinctively chose plants which appealed to him. His youth in Brazil and his travels in Indonesia and Egypt had given him an important insight, 'it is a war against hotness here'. Layered planting with tall, tough trees sheltering more delicate understoreys came naturally to him. Since those early years he has learnt a great deal by getting dirty and caring for the garden single-handedly. He describes himself as a passionate gardener who spends hours among his plants. It is the best way to learn and, as he happily points out, saves him money too.

FAR LEFT The *riad* garden is stuffed full of an exuberant collection of pomegranates, bananas, bougainvillea, plumbago and huge mounds of *Chamaerops humilis*, many of which remind Homero of his native Brazil. The old paving had perished and has been removed leaving bare brick but there are plans to replace it with the glowing green zigzags seen elsewhere in the property.

LEFT The Riad Madani is a palatial property with several open courtyards and corridors, each with its own character. This space has been treated like a little oasis pond, with a tiny island, supporting a trio of palms.

Riad Madani 59

LEFT The roof terrace at the Riad Madani is painted in the intense hue of Majorelle Blue, which complements the orange tones of a tiled wall fountain.

BELOW A wooden horseshoe arch is barely visible beneath rampant vines, while beautifully painted doors are enjoyed while they last – details which give a taste of luxury.

RIGHT *Podranea ricasoliana*, otherwise known as the Pink Trumpet Vine, has been trained to provide the perfect shady spot for lunch, complete with flowery fringe.

60 Gardens of Marrakesh

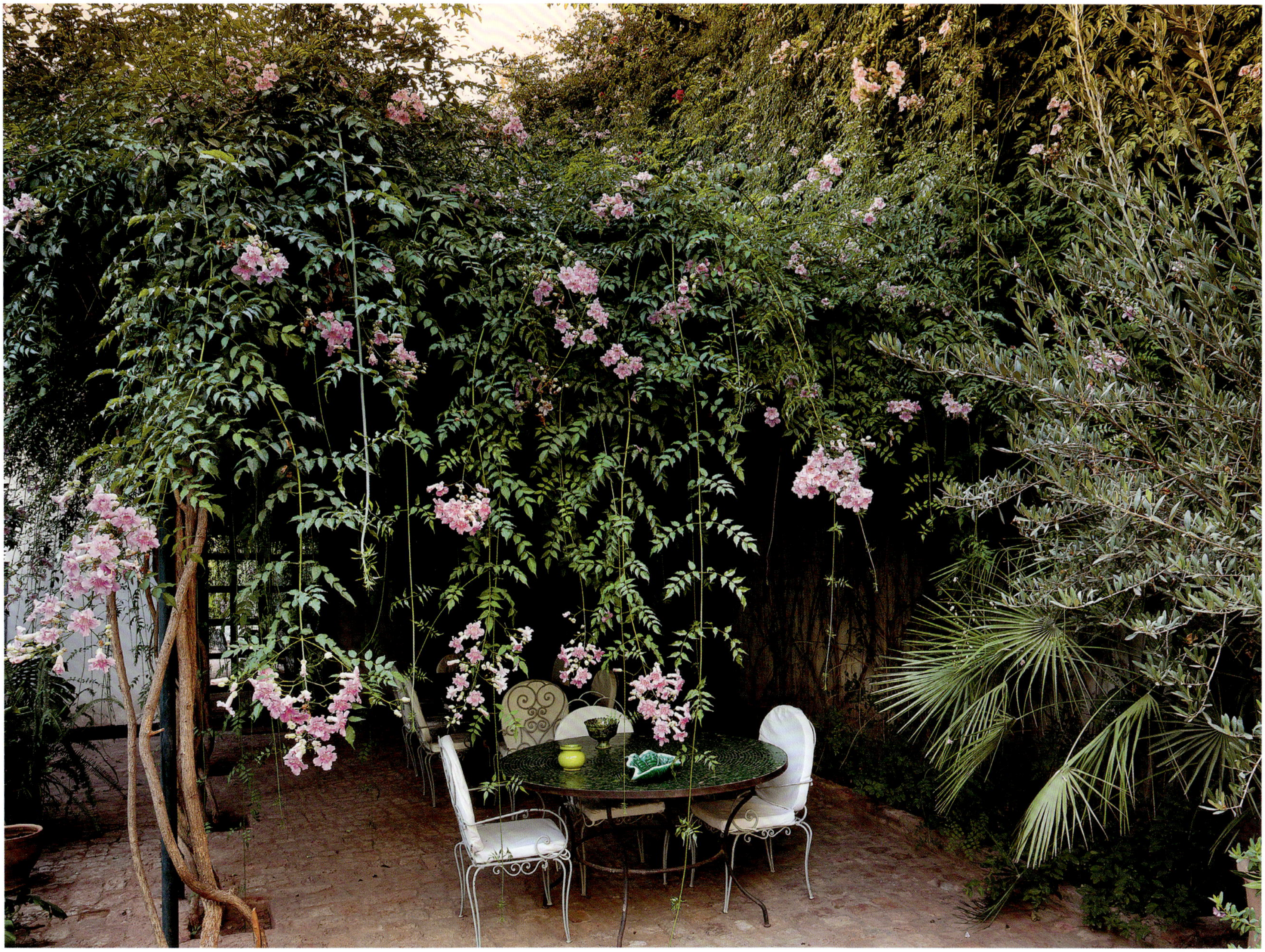

62   Gardens of Marrakesh

10. The Mamounia Gardens

LEFT The Mamounia is the *grande dame* of Marrakesh hotels and this entrance garden hits the right note of romance, luxury, fantasy and simplicity. Tiled steps edged in traditional green and white *zellij* lead indirectly up to the impressive front doors, surrounded by luxuriant planting, which is a sign of life and abundance. Oversized lanterns light the travellers' way in the tradition of Islamic hospitality.

There is no bright sign outside. It would be superfluous, a bit like Buckingham Palace announcing itself in lights. The Mamounia is not just the most notable hotel in Marrakesh but is something of a twentieth-century legend. Its guestbook, known as the *Livre d'or*, sparkles with a host of starry signatures ranging from Charlie Chaplin to Will Smith, Marlene Dietrich to Sharon Stone, Alfred Hitchcock to Martin Scorsese and General de Gaulle to Nelson Mandela. Churchill was a big fan, describing the view from his balcony as 'paintaceous', with the famous gardens being, 'the most lovely spot in the whole world'.

The Mamounia hotel and gardens occupies the 15 hectare site of an eighteenth-century princely *arsat* garden. Sultan Mohammed ben Abdallah (r.1757–90) was a cultured man who had a deep affinity for gardens, launching a vast restoration programme and constructing many new ones. He is generally credited for developing the idea of the *arsat*, a productive orchard garden including a zone of habitation, into a new garden aesthetic. Each of his four sons received one as a wedding gift and these *arsats* became known eponymously as Abdeslam, Mamoun, Moussa and Hassan. Records note the perfect symmetry of these walled gardens consisting of a wide central allée with lateral paths and transversals. Decorative kiosks and grand pavilions were sited at important junctures and the whole area was planted with productive trees such as olives and citrus, with seasonal vegetables and flowers between.

A delightful description of 1882 tells of a French archaeological delegation which was housed in the Arsat Mamoun in a pavilion almost lost in the middle of the gardens, with some of the group camped out in tents among the orange trees within reach of luscious fruit. Indeed the hotel was developed in 1923 to accommodate the growing number of European officials and a burgeoning tourist industry. The 'Art Deco meets Orientalism' design of 1922 by architects Prost and Marchisio acquired almost mythic status and subsequent renovations have always been critiqued in relation to the much loved original. The most recent of these updates closed the hotel for three years. It reopened in 2009 after the celebrated designer Jacques Garcia had remodelled nearly 80 per cent of it. Changes were made to the garden too but new interventions were designed to be discreet because, as a member of staff explains, 'the garden is our history, it gave us our name and is the soul of the hotel'.

Staying at the Mamounia is costly but non-residents are usually welcome to order a drink on the terrace and enjoy the gardens. Visitors reach the entrance via a zigzag path of gleaming *zellij* tiles, amid exotic planting decorated with enormous lanterns of coloured

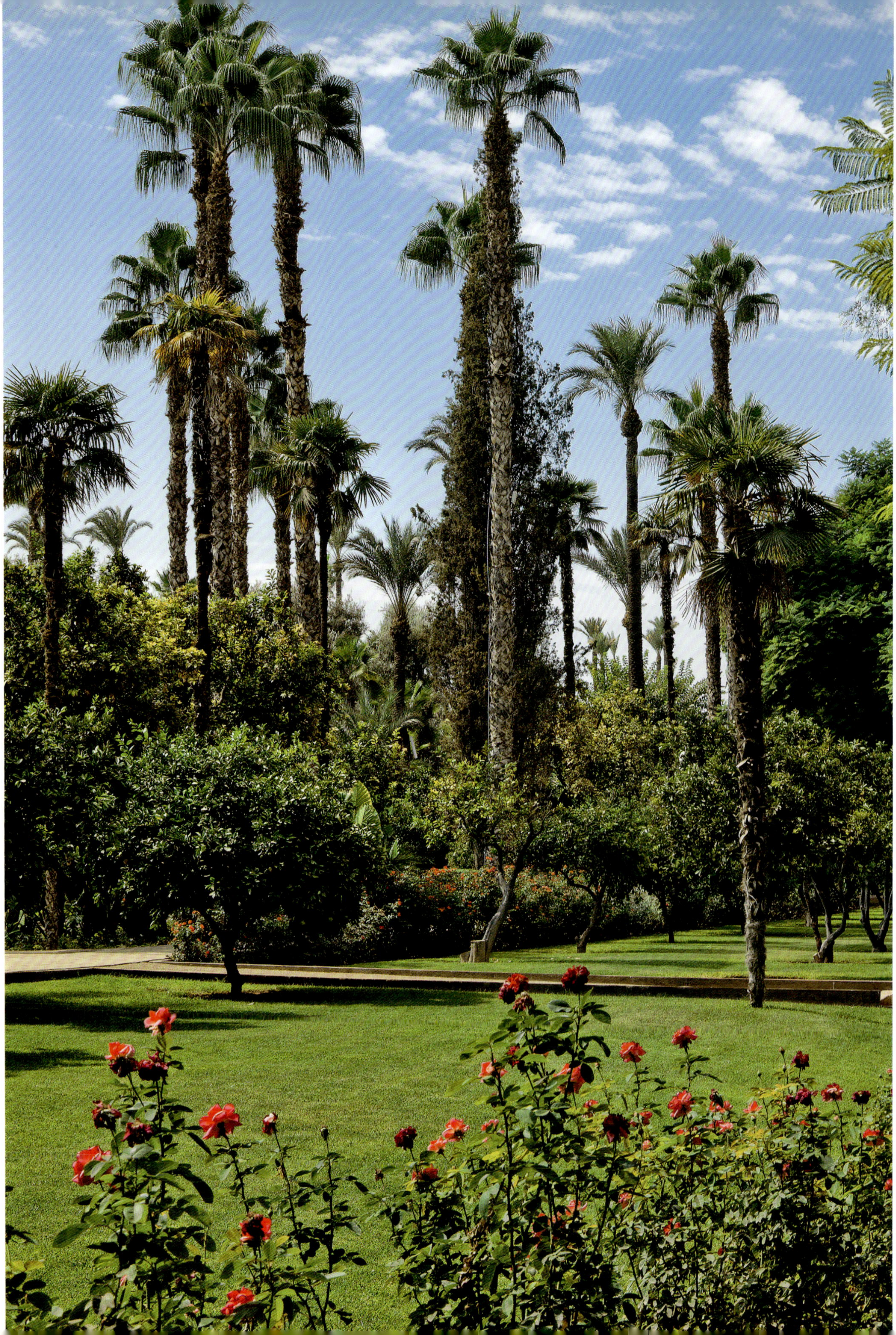

glass. The doors are swept open before you have time to think, revealing the luxurious lobby which leads through to a large terrace and the famous garden. The view is of a wide avenue of crushed pink stone lined with tall, graceful, grey-green olives, underplanted in shades of white. The effect is serene, elegant and timeless. Garcia adjusted the width of this central path so that it perfectly balances the doorway from which the garden is entered to reinforce the perspective. The lines of the old *arsat* can still be imagined in the

LEFT At the Mamounia immaculate lawns of Kikuyu grass (*Pennisetum clandestinum*) host beds of roses and six species of palm, including these date palms (*Phoenix dactylifera*) which dwarf the competition, looking like tousle-headed giants.

BELOW The old *arsat* was tucked behind the Medina walls for safety but today these same walls offer privacy and are also aesthetically pleasing. Rows of citrus trees have been planted, each within a carefully tended circle of earth, to recall something of the old *arsat* design. The 300-year-old olive tree in the foreground of the picture is one of many which would have been placed around the perimeter of large, square areas of cultivation. Today they are supplemented by beds of ornamental plants including solanum, white roses, delphinium, cosmos and canna lilies.

blocks of lawn edged with olives and roses, and filled with rows of citrus trees. The remarkably green lawns are of Kikuyu grass (*Pennisetum clandestinum*), which is well suited to harsh climates but is so vigorous that it is classified as a noxious weed in some areas. Lawns would not have appeared in the *arsat* design but they have a cooling effect on the space, providing a velvet backcloth for the fruit trees whose feet are encircled by precisely drawn skirts of bare earth. The majestic olive trees however would have certainly been a major feature of the old garden with a clutch of 800-year-old specimens predating Prince Mamoun's day showing their age in sculptural knots and twists.

Like its nearby sibling garden, the Arsat Moulay Abdeslam, the Mamounia is bounded to the west by the Medina walls. The tall, crenellated, adobe walls have been left unadorned as they have a patina of age which speaks of the gardens' historic past. The *arsat* would have been entirely shut off from the outside world by such walls but today the main building provides something of a barrier and newer walls complete the effect. These have been clothed with closely clipped bougainvillea which, when in bloom, paints the surface with a magenta glow which is an exception to the generally restrained planting palette. The one surviving eighteenth-century feature is the *menzeh* or pavilion in the centre of the garden. This has been remodelled to create a tea house for guests to relax in a secluded garden setting. Garcia felt that by locating certain facilities in the garden, such as the gymnasium and Moroccan restaurant, guests could enjoy a different experience. The requirement to accommodate the needs of hotel clients has affected the simple symmetry of the original design, but this is a living garden which, while respecting its history, has to earn its keep in the modern world. An obvious example is the necessity for an outdoor swimming pool but there are also novelties such as a fashionable cactus garden, found near the terrace, with its twenty-one species set in a landscape of boulders. Another newcomer is the *potager* to which every modern Michelin-starred chef aspires but which relates back to the site's roots as a productive garden. This kitchen garden was started three years ago and is growing in size, currently covering 1,500 square metres. It is situated at the far end of the garden and draws visitors with its range of exotic and unusual fruit, vegetables and herbs. The chef acknowledges that it will never be able to supply all the kitchen's needs but it is inspirational and allows him to add touches of interest, such as fresh citronella which is impossible to source in local markets.

As the chef talked enthusiastically about his new *potager*, life around him seemed to have a timeless quality. A young kitchen hand, bent double, gathered armfuls of fresh ingredients to fill his basket, birds sang with ardent fervour and a straw-hatted old gardener passed leisurely by, leading a donkey-drawn cart full of bougainvillea prunings, their only sound a melodic crunch on gravel. Could it be that this modern hotel garden still retains the memory of Prince Mamoun's *arsat*?

LEFT Various facilities have been sited in the garden of the Mamounia Hotel to tempt visitors outside, including the Moroccan Restaurant with its own terrace, bordered by this shimmering water feature. A rectangular pool on two levels has been designed to let the merest trickle of water from the higher pool flow in a diaphanous veil over opaline tiles to the pool below.

RIGHT A young apprentice chef enjoys a moment in the sun in the kitchen garden.

The Mamounia Gardens 67

BELOW Cyber terminals are a novel feature of this part of the park. The touch screen facility allows free access to the internet, which sponsor, Maroc Telecom, believes to be symbolic of the democratising effect of the telecommunications revolution. Planting here is a gregarious mix of classic and novel with *Chamaerops humilis* an unusual understudy to orange trees and date palms, all dressed in a skirt of ivy.

RIGHT Two magnificent specimens of the dark leaved, fast-growing, evergreen, *Ficus retusa*, the Cuban Laurel, frame the newly made basin beyond. These trees were introduced in the 1920s and have adapted wonderfully well to the Moroccan climate from their native Malaysia.

11. Arsat Moulay Abdeslam Cyber Park

When the hurly burly of the Place Jemaa el-Fna becomes too much many people retire to the upper terraces of the surrounding cafes and restaurants to seek refuge. However, for those in the know, there is a cool green alternative just a few minutes away. Anywhere with cyber in its name may conjure visions of a Silicon Valley complex of electronic workshops, but this public park is a fascinating experiment in mixing old and new: Morocco's historic past and modern future as symbolised by the telecommunications revolution.

Opened in 2005, the sparkling new park has an important history. Situated on the Avenue Mohammed V, within the rampart walls of the Medina, the eight hectare site was once a princely *arsat*, given to Prince Moulay Abdeslam in the mid eighteenth century by his father Sultan Mohammed Ben Abdallah, just as he had given

BELOW Archaeologists were surprised to find no trace of a formal water feature but the designers felt compelled to include one in the Cyber Park. They chose to build a shallow, four-part water basin, each with an island featuring a single orange tree and a multitude of graceful arching sprays. Traditional, green glazed tiles contrast beautifully with the red coloured, crushed stone used to dress the pathways; a metaphor on the power of water to green the red earth of the landscape around Marrakesh.

another son, Prince Moulay Mamoun, a similar *arsat* nearby which is now the Mamounia Hotel. Marrakesh has a complex vocabulary to describe its gardens, using both Arabic and Berber words. *Arsat, arsa* or *arset* refer to an irrigated, food producing garden, which is large but not vast, and includes a zone of habitation. Developed inside the city walls they were important in the local economy and provided fresh food and animal fodder in times of siege. Over one hundred of these unique gardens still existed in the early 1900s, but they were systematically consumed by urban development before it was realised that they should have been protected. This loss to the garden-city can be clearly seen on a modern map where new residential areas ironically bear the old names of the *arsats* which they destroyed.

In the 1920s the *arsat* Moulay Abdeslam was remodelled to suit French taste, including wide avenues, carpet bedding and a plethora of exotica, which was all the rage at the time. After Independence in 1956 the site deteriorated until by the 1980s it had largely been abandoned by any responsible body. The local population appropriated the area for a variety of uses including a football pitch, a funfair, a practice ground for the acrobats working the Jemaa el-Fna, and other less salubrious activities. All that remained of the former gardens were a number of trees struggling to stay alive. This prime site seemed set to become another victim of developers, in this case hoping to build a luxury hotel. Fortunately this potential tragedy was averted at the last moment and the site was dedicated as a public green space.

This important place offered several design opportunities: to create a new park for the twenty-first century, restore the old *arsat*, or recreate the Protectorate plan. In the end it was a bit of all three, due to an unusual partnership between the Foundation Mohammed VI for the Protection of the Environment, the City of Marrakesh and Maroc Telecom, along with other commercial investors such as Sony Ericsson. The deal was that Maroc Telecom would pay for the refurbishment and upkeep of the park to the standards set by the Foundation in exchange for the commercial right to exploit part of the site as a multi-media and cyber-space exhibition area and theatre. The Foundation insisted that the restoration should be in the spirit of the original so as to merit the label 'historic garden'. They also stated that there should be an environmental project associated with any new space and that it would be both a tourist attraction as well as being open to all levels of society. For Maroc Telecom the park would showcase modernity and be symbolic of the democratic nature of the telecommunications revolution.

Architect Karim El Achak and landscape designer Jean-Charles Mazet were given the job of reconciling these sometimes conflicting goals. The solution they arrived at was a compromise: they would restore part of the old *arsat*, reconfigure the Protectorate Garden to include the modern telecommunications elements, and create a buffer zone between the two consisting of relaxing lawns set with trees. Meticulous research, including a dendrological survey, revealed the original features of the gardens. In the *arsat* it was discovered that the surviving 300-year-old olive trees delineated approximate squares of cultivation, or were placed in alignment within blocks, with spaces in between large enough to be inter-planted with seasonal vegetables. The designers restored old pathways using sand and *terre battu*, a traditional technique of beaten earth. These were raised well above the planted areas to increase the effect of a *jardin décaissé*, or broken up garden, which, while recalling the layout of more sophisticated gardens such as that of the Bahia Palace, is essentially a practical device for making irrigation more effective. Having identified the general shape of the *arsat* any extra vegetation, which included mimosa, acacia, robinia, fig and lilac, was stripped away. Young olives were inter-planted to complete rows, with seasonal vegetables between, and oranges, lemons and mandarins. The result is a garden of exceptional serenity, perfumed, sober and cool. It was important to save this unique garden type, for historic interest, but perhaps more importantly, for future generations to better appreciate the sophistication of their garden heritage.

The Protectorate garden however was valued more for its botanical strengths and it was deemed justifiable to superimpose modern elements on its design. In contrast to the gentle, rustic charm of the *arsat* the modern garden is highly decorative and confident with its wide avenues, majestic trees, exotic shrubs, plants and 'cyber' features. It is stimulating and sensuous, offering a bolder palette of form and colour, with new structural elements in steel and glass punctuating the whole with novelty and surprise. The mandatory telecommunications museum and commercial sales point is sited right on the margin of the park, serving as a light-infused glass portal. The elegant interactive terminals with their round bases and matching roofs are placed carefully like herms for the space age. Their purpose is to give educational information about the park, its history and botany, as well as standard internet facilities, free of charge. Symbolically this facility represents the desire to make the telecommunications revolution freely accessible to all, but in reality it seems to attract mainly gaggles of young people passing time.

Sandwiched between these competing aesthetics is the buffer zone which seems timeless in its simplicity. Venerable stands of

BELOW LEFT Careful study revealed squares of cultivation, often edged with olive trees, containing rows of citrus and other fruit trees, alternated with ribbons of seasonal vegetables or alfalfa. In the new Cyber Park fountain grass is used to define the plots with a soft and flexible border. It is trimmed back in winter to its denser core.

BELOW RIGHT When in flower, the feathery panicles of *Pennisetum setaceum* shimmer in the breeze, like glittering sprays of water, engendering its common name, Fountain Grass.

RIGHT Irrigation in the *arsat* follows traditional methods, with areas of cultivation, separated into sections by small earth dams, flooded in rotation. The result is practical but can also create a mirror-like, reflective surface which adds another dimension to the scene.

palm trees have been given space on a pool of greensward and look rather like living sculpture, some rocketing high into the sky and other multi-stemmed specimens creating muscular groups on bulbous bases. The little irrigation dams called *seguia* are to be found throughout the planting areas, but here their graceful curves add a calligraphic element, like flowing script, to the balance of the composition, taking us both forward and backward in time.

The park works on many worthy levels, fulfilling its ideological, cultural and technical brief. It is a beacon for other projects which aim to preserve the green heritage of the city both in its historical integrity and financial master plan. What is most striking however is that people enjoy this place where they can meet, mix, wander in poetic solitude or simply breathe. It is probably one of the city's best kept secrets.

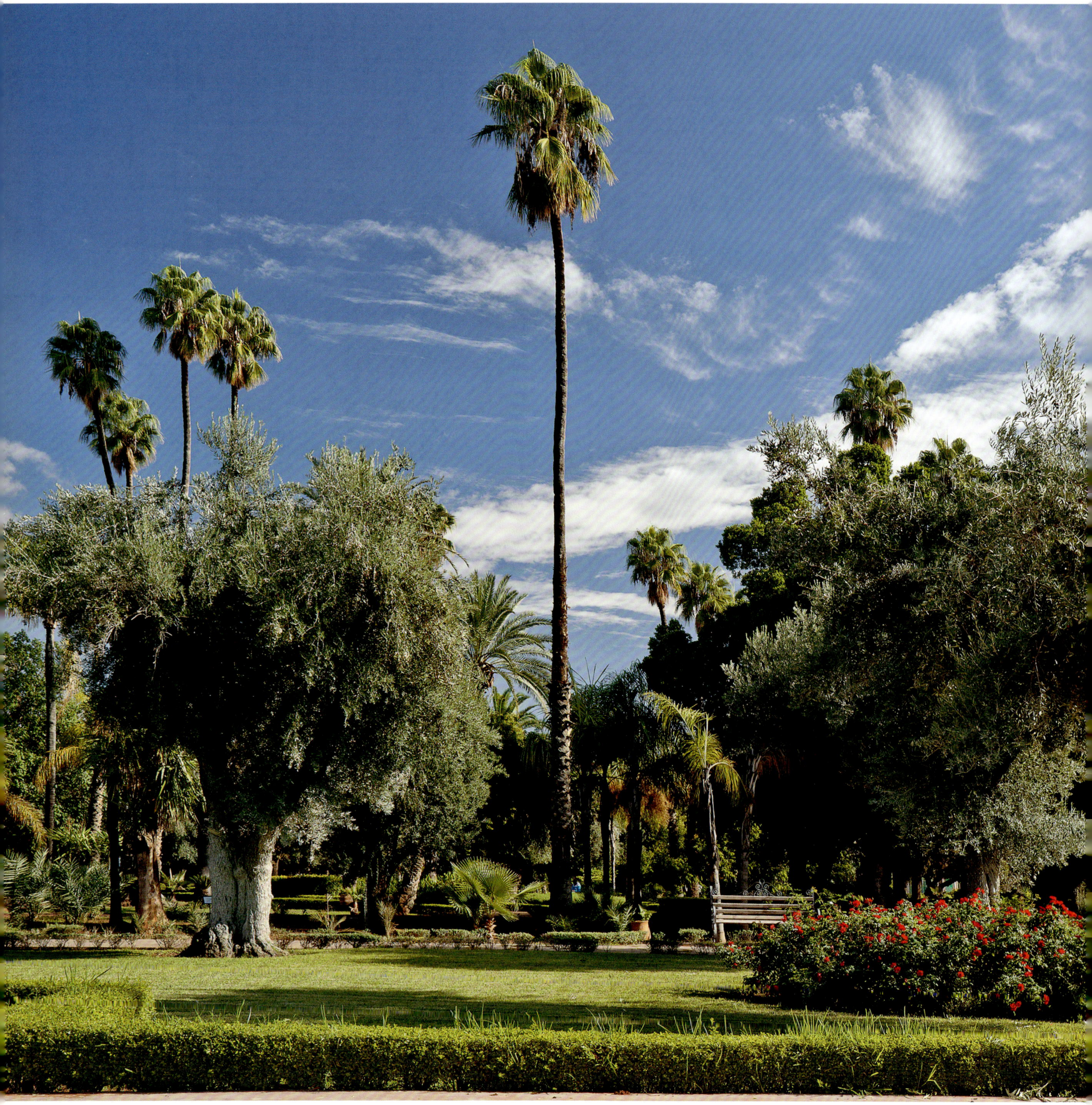

12. Jnane el Harti

LEFT The wide avenues, extensive open areas and big skies of the park come as welcome relief from the intensity of city life.

It takes time to recover from the indignities of colonialism, and during that process it is sometimes difficult to know quite how to deal with its cultural legacy, including its gardens. When George Orwell visited Marrakesh in 1939 he came to recuperate from tuberculosis. During his stay he wrote the novel *Coming up for Air* and an interesting essay, 'Marrakesh', which is a mordant lambaste of colonial attitudes. The essay makes for uncomfortable reading except for one short passage: 'I was feeding one of the gazelles in the public gardens. Gazelles are almost the only animals that look good to eat when they are still alive, in fact, one can hardly look at their hindquarters without thinking of mint sauce.' That public garden was the recently-built Jnane el Harti in the French New Town.

The gardens were created in the early 1930s as part of a new urban plan, developed from 1913 by the architect Léon-Henri Prost. The French ruling authority decreed that all new building development should take place beyond the historic centre. The idea was to preserve the old city but it resulted in a physical separation of the population which reinforced socio-economic and cultural differences. Prost attempted to ameliorate the situation by creating the Avenue Mohammed V, which links the New Town with the Medina. The gardens are situated off this avenue, near the busy Place 16 Novembre, between the two main areas of the New Town, the Guéliz and the Hivernage. The design follows the lines of any French park of the era with large sweeps of lawn and trees for shade. A goose foot arrangement of avenues, linked by meandering paths, ends in a central plaza off which there are other, more intimate, areas. Painted-trellis arbours, trained with roses and honeysuckle, and decorative metal benches would have been comfortably familiar to new French residents.

However, Prost was interested in local architectural idioms and consciously took account of them in his work (which included a plan for Istanbul). The adoption of the term *jnane* is a clue to the desire to create a space which is relevant to its setting. *Jnane* is an Arabic word which describes the heavenly garden of Paradise in the Koran. It came to denote a specific garden form, which had to include fruit trees, palms and grape vines. Clearly this is not the case at the Jnane el Harti but the choice of name shows sensitivity towards Islamic culture, even if the design is confusing. The park was always intended to welcome a wide spectrum of users and, in an effort to be inclusive, several built features were designed to be familiar to the local population. The bandstand in the middle of the plaza is a version of a *menzeh* or open-sided pavilion. To one side of the plaza is a water feature based on Islamic design principles, with tiled canals, carved stone basins and water jets. Behind the bandstand is a peaceful little garden designed around two dovecotes, but these are replicas of adobe watchtowers built by Berber people to survey routes from the Sahara. The *pigeonnier* (dovecote) is emblematic of the French, rural good-life: the bigger the *pigeonnier* the more affluent the household. It is difficult to know if there was any thought given to the possible symbolic significance of these proud watchtowers being transformed into deluxe homes for pigeons.

The Harti remained almost unchanged for several decades. It shrank somewhat in size and the gazelles disappeared, but it continued to be a local park where retired bureaucrats read their newspapers and mothers strolled with their young children. However by 2002 it was showing signs of neglect and a programme to give it a complete facelift was launched and funded by the City Council of Marrakesh and the International Association of Francophone Mayors.

LEFT A mature Canary Island Palm (*Phoenix canariensis*) dwarfs the bandstand set in a large open space in the centre of the park at Jnane el Harti. The awkward design shows a desire to imbue French Art Deco style with a bit of local colour which, in this case, has had a rather unhappy outcome.

RIGHT Town planner Prost was intrigued by Berber architecture and chose to model his *pigeonnier*, or dovecote, on the rammed earth watch towers they made in the High Atlas Mountains. The originals are still impressive today and are more rustic and monumental than Prost's rather polite version.

This latter organisation is a forum for exchange and support on a number of issues for local mayors in French-speaking countries. One of the aims of the association is to support cultural projects including the restoration of historic gardens and the greening of urban spaces in general. That being so there would have been no question of allowing landscape architect Souad Belkziz a free hand to make radical change. Basically his brief was to make the existing park better. He put in new automatic, water-saving irrigation systems and good lighting. Many period features such as the pergolas, benches and signage were beautifully restored or replaced with copies. The major structural elements were made to look new and avenues and paths were resurfaced in hardwearing materials.

It is the choice of new plant material which is the most interesting feature of the renovation, creating a new more relevant site. This is the result of collaboration between knowledgeable, local nurserymen and horticultural experts sponsored by the office of the Mayor of Paris. The municipality of Marrakesh shows no resistance to seeking advice when appropriate, confident in their independent vision for the city. The team introduced many new species, upgrading the park to look more like a botanic garden. Some of the old bedding schemes have been replaced by drifts of grasses, creating a softer, modern, dreamy effect. In other areas mixed perennials and annuals have been arranged in meadow-like array, their jewel colours resembling Persian rugs. The park is well furnished with beautiful mature palm trees, which are a unifying feature, and these have been interspersed with various short varieties such as Lady Palm (*Rhapis excelsa*). Areas of cactus have been created, showing off the range of species which, while not being native, are well suited to the climate zone. Beautiful, mature olive trees are pruned to celebrate their natural form in contrast to formal clipped hedges and topiary. Overall the new park has retained its formal bones but these have been overlaid with planting which looks to the future. Gradually the park is finding a different voice, one which accepts its colonial origins but is speaking for a modern Marrakesh.

RIGHT ABOVE Pergolas, like this one, laden with Pink Trumpet Vine (*Podranea ricasoliana*) are pretty features at Jnane el Harti which date from the 1930s. The surrounding flower beds however are changing in character to reflect the modern concern for water conservation. Drought tolerant species, such as this clump of *Aloe vera*, whose spiky blooms resemble those of *Kniphofia*, are increasingly de rigueur.

RIGHT BELOW Whole areas of the park are being re-landscaped to reduce the burden of thirsty lawns and bedding plants. Here, a boulder path winds its way through a new plantation of exotics from Mesoamerica, including *Beaucarnia recurvata*, the Ponytail Palm, which is not really a palm at all. It has a strange bottle shaped caudex, or swollen trunk, in which it stores water.

78 Gardens of Marrakesh

BELOW Layers of shapes, textures and colours work wonderfully well against a brilliant blue sky with the bright foliage of the variegated Indian Laurel, *Ficus retusa nitida* 'Variegata', looking like splashes of sunshine.

Jnane el Harti

80 Gardens of Marrakesh

13. Jardin Majorelle

LEFT This unusual view of the world famous Majorelle garden illustrates the huge botanical variety in this relatively small site. Exaggerated verticals and expansive horizontals create a dynamic tension which gives the design surreal overtones.

BELOW This sense of the weird and wonderful can be seen in microcosm in the details of individual plants like this barrel cactus whose starburst spines glow bright red.

The Majorelle is one of the glories of Marrakesh. Prepare your senses by arriving by *calèche*, one of the horse-drawn carriages whose drivers negotiate the traffic with the skill of a Roman charioteer. The garden may be small, less than half a hectare, but it packs a big punch with its series of mini landscapes taking the visitor on an unforgettable sensory journey from cool dreamy calm to hot prickly frisson.

The eponymous garden is the *chef-d'œuvre* of Jacques Majorelle, painter, plant collector and scholarly enthusiast for the culture of Marrakesh and the Sahara region. Born in Nantes in 1886, the son of the celebrated Art Nouveau furniture designer Louis Majorelle, he trained as an artist at the Académie Julian in Paris. His first visit to Marrakesh in 1917 was to prove momentous, the start of a lifelong love affair, and in 1924 he purchased a plot of land outside the city walls in the Guéliz, known as Bousafsaf, which translates as 'place where poplar trees grow'. The Moorish-style villa which he built there is now known as the Villa Oasis, but the garden we see today occupies an adjacent plot on which Majorelle commissioned a rigidly geometric modernist studio, designed by the French architect Paul Sinon in 1931. This was where he indulged his two passions, painting and gardening, creating a botanic wonderland intended to delight and astonish. He opened it to the public in 1947.

The basic design of the garden is free-form, rather like an exotic Victorian shrubbery, with red-painted concrete paths which meander through planting in a series of loops. However, this is far from a typical European garden: there are no lawns, avenues or axial views as in the French Protectorate style of the day. Instead Majorelle created a personal idiom, blending elements of the local Islamic tradition with his artistic vision in which the garden is developed as a series of unfolding, living canvases, each eliciting its own emotion. An element of surprise and contradiction is ever present making this a sensuous place rather than a spiritual Islamic courtyard or a garden of controlled grandeur. The visitor moves from the eerie beauty of a cool bamboo forest, its elegant culms filtering a lime-green light, through areas of squat fan palms and agaves set among towering date palms, to a cactus garden of horrid fascination, beyond which is a lily pool of Monet-like beauty. Water is a key element, as it is throughout the region, with a surprisingly formal canal driving a geometric line through the gentle curves, and large square pools and fountains cooling and animating the space with their sound and reflections. Kiosks and pavilions provide architectural points of interest and shelter from the fierce summer sun.

But the single most influential choice Majorelle made was to adopt a striking cobalt blue which he had come across in his travels

Jardin Majorelle 81

82   Gardens of Marrakesh

LEFT The vibrant, saturated hue of Majorelle Blue is both the defining and unifying element of the garden. It provides a backdrop for three much photographed, iconic combinations: the yellow 'egg' pot with purple *Tradescantia pallida*, the similarly coloured, wide-shouldered pot with the silver 'elephant ears' of *Kalanchoe beharensis* and the wide-mouthed pot with *Justicia candicans*, known as the Shrimp Plant.

Jardin Majorelle 83

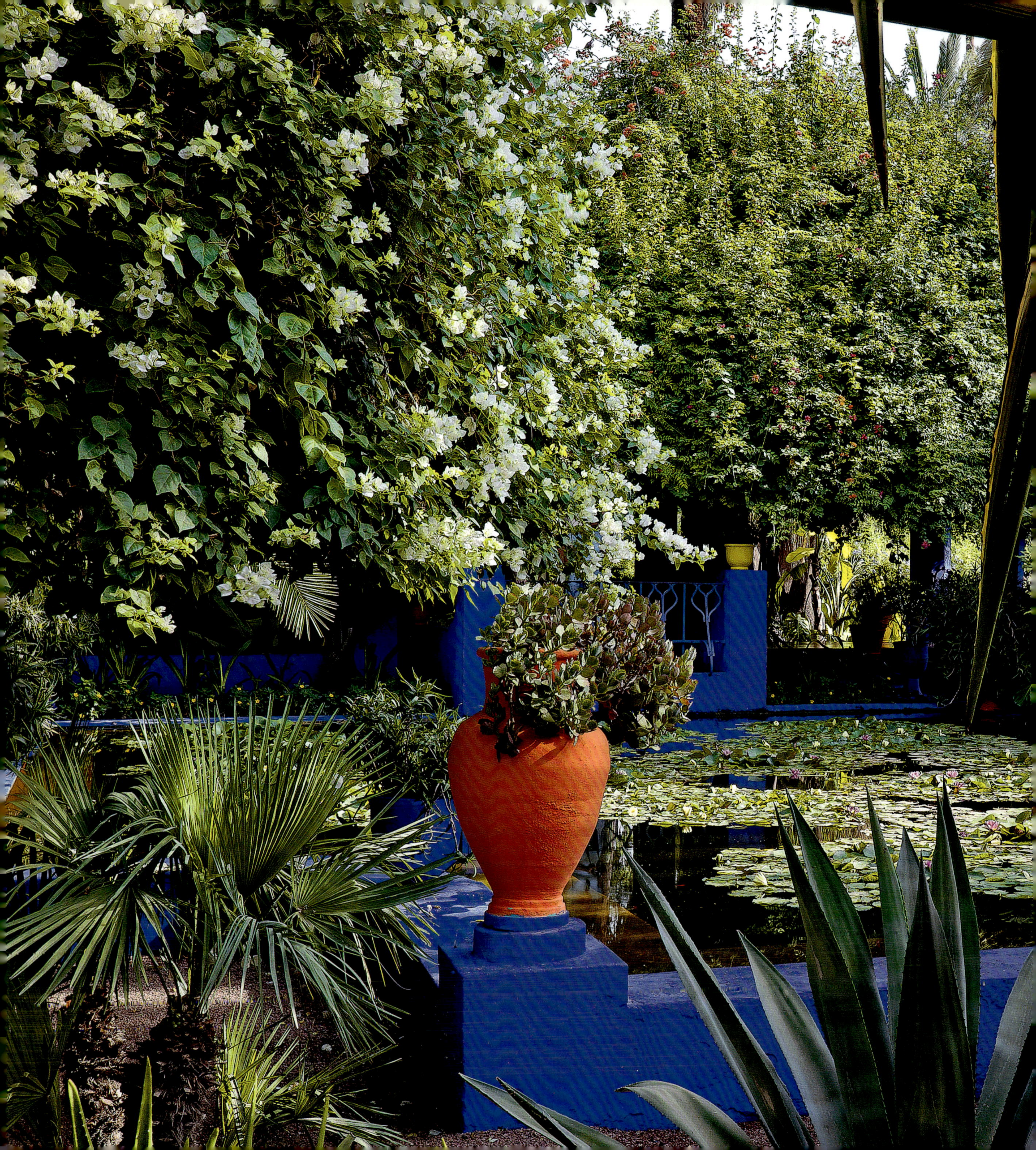

LEFT The lily pool is pure Monet by Matisse, with the pastel shades of the waterlilies being upstaged by the rampant exuberance of a cacophony of different exotic species, all kept in their place by Majorelle's blue.

Jardin Majorelle 85

RIGHT The tray-sized, glossy leaves of *Monstera deliciosa* lie prostrate here, at the edge of the bamboo grove but elsewhere the plant reveals its true nature as a vine, cladding tree trunks in a leathery sheath for up to twenty metres.

BELOW A simple bamboo balustrade makes a bridge out of a red-stained concrete path through a grove of giant bamboo. Painted pots in yellow, powder blue, pistachio, orange and Majorelle Blue mark one's progress through this limelit jungle.

FAR RIGHT Majorelle was particularly fond of cacti and Yves Saint Laurent and Pierre Bergé have extended his collection to include spectacular specimens from all over the Americas. Four-ribbed, columnar *Cereus peruvianus*, seen to the left in the foreground and again in the background, can reach a height of over five metres, while the similar but slower growing *Pachycereus pringlei* is fatter and sprouts the occasional side branch.

86 Gardens of Marrakesh

in the Berber villages of the South. In what must have seemed an act of sheer aesthetic madness he painted the exterior of his studio (and most of the garden structures), in this exhilarating hue, which famously came to be known as Majorelle Blue. Terracotta pots were given the same treatment, but with an extended palette of orange, citrus yellow and pale blue adding exciting highlights of colour to what is essentially a composition in shades of green. It is the masterly control of bold colour, form and emotion which elevates the Majorelle to the realms of a great garden.

The garden remained open after the death of its creator in 1962, attracting visitors despite its increasingly unkempt state, among whom were the French couturier Yves Saint Laurent and his partner Pierre Bergé. Their first visit in 1966 was the beginning of an extraordinary relationship with the site which they visited on a regular basis until, in 1980, they bought the Villa Oasis. Shortly afterwards they acquired the Jardin Majorelle itself, saving it from destruction by speculators. In the year 2000 they endowed the garden with substantial funds for a complete restoration under the direction of the American landscape designer Madison Cox and the Moroccan ethnobotanist Abderrazzak Benchaabane, who was given responsibility for the planting.

Benchaabane describes his approach as painterly, in the spirit of Majorelle. Eschewing plans and diagrams he spent many hours observing the garden in different lights and seasons, intuitively placing plants to greatest effect. Original structural elements were renovated but much of the planting, with the exception of large trees, was renewed. The diversity of species, of which Majorelle was so proud, has been extended to represent five continents, with Benchaabane adding touches of floral interest. The sculptural quality of specimen plants has been enhanced by setting them in their own space and covering the ground between with a layer of immaculately raked gravel, rather like a Zen garden. Twenty gardeners work full time to present a picture-perfect effect. This level of care, investment and attention to detail would be remarkable in any garden but in the difficult conditions of Marrakesh it is particularly striking. The garden is home to many birds, terrapins and fish, whose presence add another dimension to the splendour of the flora.

This is a world-class garden, unique in its genre, and a remarkable example of how a creator's vision can be understood, fostered and taken forward sympathetically beyond the lifetime of the originator. It is fitting that a small area has been dedicated as a memorial to Yves Saint Laurent who had requested that his ashes be buried in the garden he loved.

88 Gardens of Marrakesh

14. The Palais Rhoul

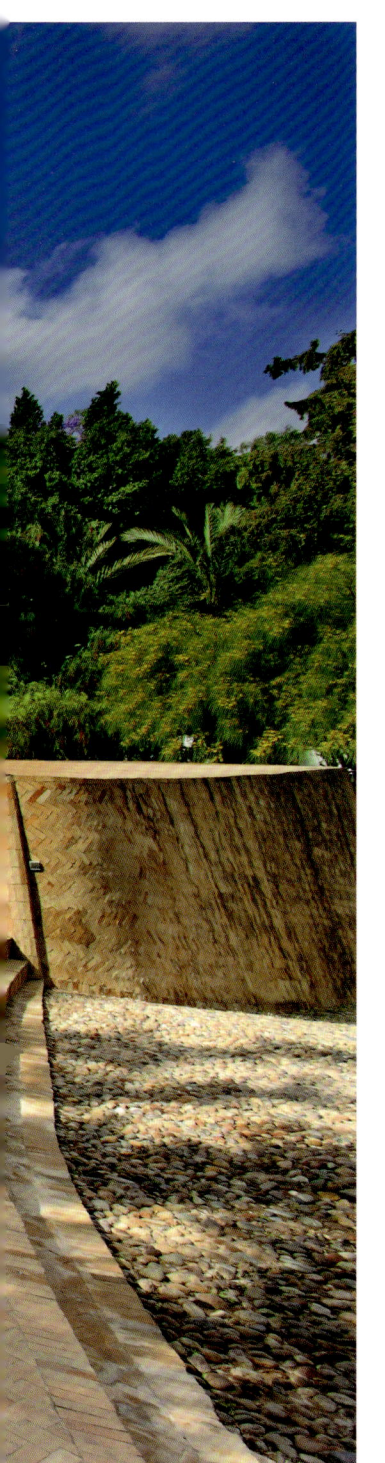

LEFT A swirl of pleated brick steps leads up to a stage-like platform from which a tiny square pool sends a strict little rill down towards the entrance door. This could easily be the set for a grand, old-style, Hollywood film, full of glamorous eastern promise.

BELOW Massive wooden gates protect the property from the proximity of the street.

Marrakesh is a city of surprises where unexpected juxtapositions stimulate the imagination and shake up the Cartesian mindset of European visitors. The Palais Rhoul is a luxury guest house set on a tree-lined street in the Palmery. With its bougainvillea-clad walls, imposing gateways and well-tended verges, this is clearly an upmarket enclave for the wealthy. However, this vision of order and exclusivity is suddenly disrupted by the arrival of a flock of sheep, which fill the street with their shaggy bulk and grumbling cries. Driven by an elderly shepherd, whose weathered features and serene gait have a timeless quality, they are a reminder that the Palmery is a shared space where a traditional, semi-rural way of life still exists alongside the villas of newcomers.

Considered to be something of a stately elder among these newcomers, the Palais Rhoul contains its fair share of surprises too. The heavily studded wooden entrance gates open onto a short straight drive, lined with dumpy Canary Island palms, looking like a row of overfed soldiers with huge, ceremonial, feathered helmets. This ends abruptly at an unusual proscenium-like structure, built in biscuit-coloured *bejmat* (small local bricks) and accessed by a curved sweep of steps which are broad at one side, tapering away to practically nothing at the other. The effect is uncomfortable, forcing a crab-like climb to the top from where two square pools, linked by a rill, lead down an incline to the entrance of the main building. The design of this feature is strict and monumental, its severity emphasised by the absence of plants, except for a few papyrus in the pools. It appears unwelcoming, as does the plain façade, topped by twin cupolas decorated in a fleshy pink colour like a surreal pair of breasts. There seems to be no choice but to enter the building.

The architecture is extraordinary: a luxurious hallway gives onto a huge oval space with a colonnaded, rectangular pool at its centre, flanked by the soaring inverted hemispheres of the cupolas, supported on yet more columns. The floor is tiled in a zigzag pattern of burnt orange, brown and cream, the walls and columns dressed in ivory *tadelakt*, and the pool is surrounded by glossy black marble streaked with thick white veins. Rows of old books line the shelves, objects and paintings abound and rugs and overstuffed furniture offer islands of cosiness. The vast space is glazed on three sides, so the exterior blends with the interior, carried on a flood of natural light, with indoor plants echoing the presence of their outdoor relatives. There are shelves lined with all the paraphernalia of an old family home. The uncertainty felt just a few moments before gives way to pleasure as the realisation dawns that this place is all about sophisticated fantasy – an invitation to a Pompeian house party.

LEFT The main sitting-room at the Palais Rhoul is also like something from an epic film: a bold, luxurious, confident statement of wealth, seasoned with a soupçon of self-deprecating humour.

BELOW Pass through to the rear of the building and a breathtaking sight awaits the visitor. The circular heated swimming pool is lined with pink *tadelakt* which gives the water an unearthly azure colour. Pink Trumpet Vines have been planted in containers on the roof and allowed to cascade over the parapet to form a living gauze curtain.

RIGHT Mature jacaranda trees, planted forty years ago as tender young things by the present owner, explode the very air around them with the saturated colour of their violet-blue blooms.

The Rhoul family are originally from the north-east of Morocco but bought the five hectare site in the 1950s as a retreat from their high-octane business life in Paris. They built a modest holiday home for themselves and concentrated on the pleasures of gardening, planting many of the magnificent trees which have reached maturity today. In 1994 however they opened their house to paying guests, having commissioned the Moroccan architect Aziz Lamghari to create a suitably impressive mansion. Lamghari is known for his love of what he describes as, 'the architecture of grandiose civilisations, particularly Hellenic, Persian and the Egypt of the Pharaohs'. Known for his powerful imagination and flights of fancy he has gained the epithet 'The Pillar Man', and indeed his design for the Palais Rhoul includes 180 pillars belonging to no particular order. His love affair with pillars spills out into the garden where he has created the most striking feature of the site, a round swimming pool, embraced by colonnaded terraces and a circular pavilion which forms the focal point of the design. The pool is lined with pink *tadelakt* which gives the water a beautiful, iridescent azure blue colour, its shallow edges allowing the water to purl gently onto the brink of the terrace. Pink Trumpet Vine (*Podranea ricasoliana*) trails down from the top of the colonnades forming a delicate tracery sprinkled with pink and violet bell-shaped flowers. The result teeters on the edge of Hollywood kitsch but is just restrained enough to be a serious visual treat.

Behind the pavilion the terrain swells up to an oasis of green, gently undulating lawn, dotted with tall, sheltering palms and olive trees. Luxury tents have been placed judiciously in this landscape, as if in an encampment among desert dunes which have been magically transformed into a green paradise. Blocks of trees and shrubs have been designed to create pockets of privacy. At first sight these could be in any European garden but the flashes of red on a three metre high bush are not rhododendron flowers but belong to a poinsettia. For anyone from colder climes this is an unsettlingly large version of its potted cousin, ubiquitous at Christmas time. A large stand of deciduous trees are also familiar enough except for the magnificent sweep of vivid blue high in the canopy which reveals them to be mature jacarandas. This juxtaposition of the familiar and surprising continues throughout the gardens. In an area known as the VIP garden formal island beds of roses have been cut into the lawn but have been associated with the silk floss tree (*Ceiba speciosa*), a member of the baobab family, whose green trunk can photosynthesise and is covered in strange conical thorns which store water for use in periods of drought. It is both fascinating and scary, a tree which is worthy of the imagination of Hieronymus Bosch.

The Palais Rhoul is theatrical, unapologetically quirky, and very much the result of a family ethos which seems never to do things by half. It is the perfect setting for anyone wanting to play at being a pasha or a Roman consul and indeed has hosted many actors such as Tom Cruise and Leonardo DiCaprio. In a city of surprises it still manages to hold its own.

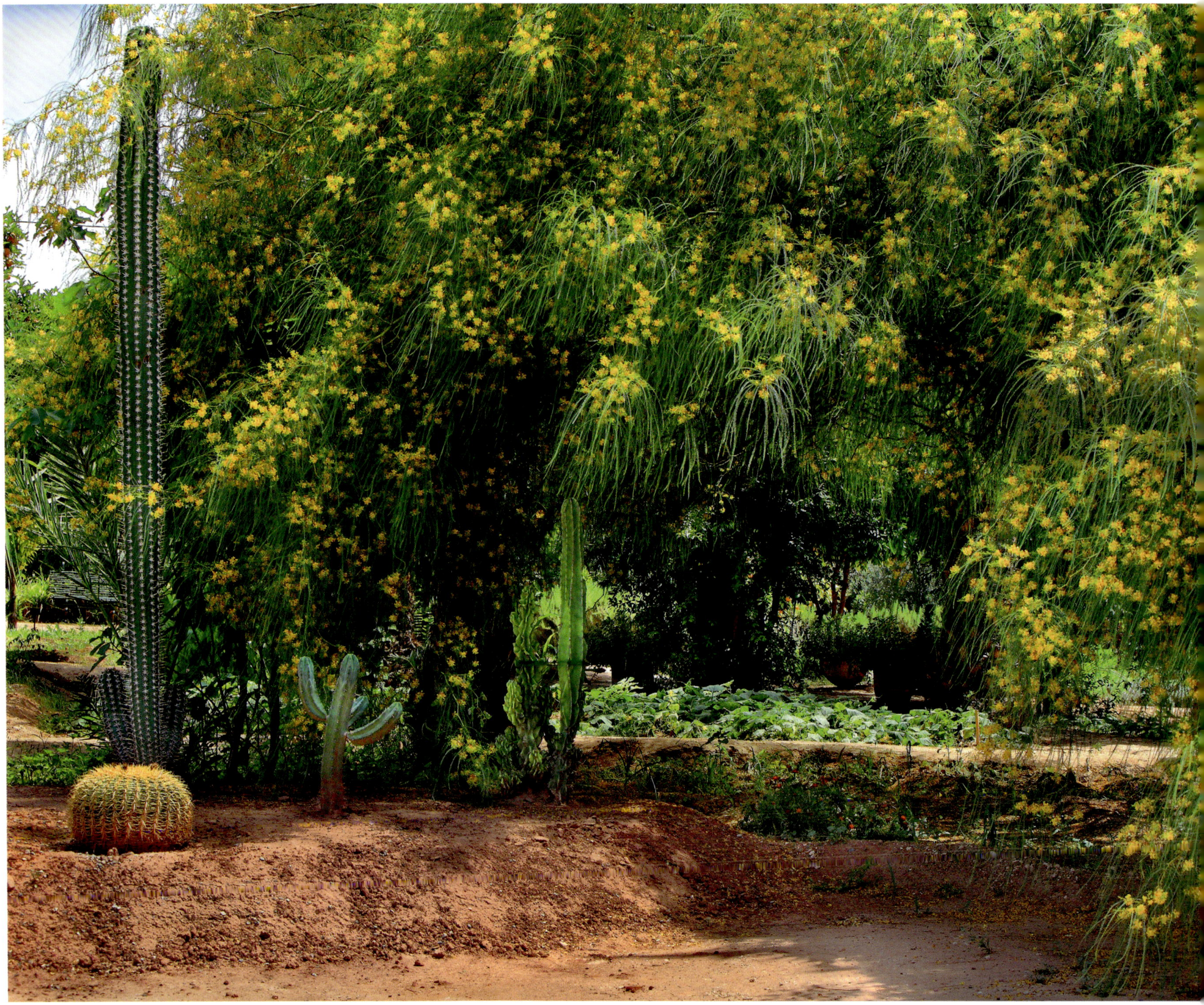

15. Les Deux Tours

The scene is almost biblical: a dusty track, palm trees and a cluster of humble dwellings whose inhabitants perform the age old rituals of daily life accompanied by a scattering of sheep and a donkey. Enter the twin-towered gateway of Les Deux Tours, created by the celebrated architect Charles Boccara, and the contrast is stark, perhaps even a little uncomfortable. However, this green oasis is not one of the Hollywood-style villas which have sprung up all over the Palmery but was conceived as an integrated extension of the traditional hamlet or *douar*, a source of work and inspiration.

Boccara is a remarkable man. Born in 1940, of Tunisian origin but brought up in Morocco, he chose to set up his practice in the Red City because, as he puts it, 'I was lazy – there was no architect working here and I would not have to fight for commissions'. This self-deprecation belies the fact that his aesthetic, which blends traditional artisanship with modern convenience, has gained him star status as one of the originators of Marrakesh Style. He describes himself as being at the service of his clients, the mainspring of his creativity being in the response to the brief. So when he and an associate bought this three hectare plot in 1991 he found it helpful to invent a brief on the theme of a little village set in a magical landscape. In 2008 the original property was renovated and extended and is now a peaceful hotel just a fifteen-minute drive from the city.

The gardens are the main event at Les Deux Tours, where nature seems to flow through the buildings in a seamless fashion, linking the series of villas, taking the visitor on a promenade of discovery. Boccara designed the garden in a series of zones each with its own personality but with a common identity that binds them, rather like members of the same family. The sinuous lines of the design, with its luxuriant lawns and relaxed planting, may appear quite European in conception. However, it is based on the Islamic tradition of discretion, where intimate spaces are revealed consecutively. Thus the little garden which welcomes the visitor is scribed by a path which turns to approach the foyer at a forty-five degree angle. This device slows the tempo so there is time to absorb the calm atmosphere, notice the colour and texture of olives, palms, oranges, cactus and hibiscus, and breathe in the perfume of honeysuckle and jasmine. Once inside, the décor of cream *tadelakt* walls and sage green paintwork is simple, allowing a visual partnership with the garden beyond.

It is almost as if the garden itself is the living space with interiors acting in a supporting role. This is not a garden of powerful vistas or thrusting design features. It seeks rather to seduce, using familiar elements in a gentle way. A twenty metre long canal is a strong design statement as one enters the garden, but it has a completely

FAR LEFT An amusing arrangement of cacti, including the wittily named Mother-in-Law's-Cushion (foreground, far left) marks the entrance to the *potager*, which includes a variety of shade-giving trees, such as this glorious Jerusalem Thorn (*Parkinsonia aculeata*).

LEFT The pool is screened by walls of pink, rammed-earth which imitate the remains of an ancient monument. Bougainvillea, seen to the left of the picture, is available in nearly every shade, including this rather zingy tangerine.

LEFT AND BELOW While pools in the garden at Les Deux Tours are formal in shape they are all planted in an understated, naturalistic style, featuring primrose-coloured waterlilies and sheaves of *Cyperus papyrus*.

BELOW Hammock or brass bed? Siesta time is a serious business.

different character to the highly coloured one at the Majorelle. Here formal geometry is counterbalanced by natural stone, lemon-coloured waterlilies, papyrus reeds and boulders covered by a cloak of green algae, from which dozens of terrapins plop into the water at the sound of a passer-by. Formal channelled waterways are also a common feature of the design lexicon in Marrakesh. At Les Deux Tours they are naturalised into a series of small rills which lace through areas of planting, forming mini cascades as they respond to changes of levels or debouch into a still pool. Areas of greensward create visually cooling washes of colour, heightening the experience of an oasis in the desert. These lawns of broad-leaved grass, adapted to the climate, are dotted with brass four-poster beds dressed in white muslin – an invitation to a romantic daydream in an unusual version of a nomad's tent.

Beyond the tiny secret walled courtyards and gently undulating gardens of delight is the potager – a decorative vegetable garden.

LEFT The head gardener at Les Deux Tours takes a moment to admire his tomatoes which he has safely supported on a lyrical scaffold of bamboo.

BELOW Attention is given to every detail and even the garden shed has its own mini garden.

96   Gardens of Marrakesh

Mathieu Boccara, son of Charles, explains that there are three elements at the heart of any settlement: shelter, protection and food. The vegetable garden therefore has a place of honour at Les Deux Tours as one in this trilogy of needs. It is roughly wheel-shaped with a large shady tree at its hub. In a Western garden this circle would usually be divided by 'spokes' creating segments of equal size, but here planting areas have been defined by winding irregular paths of beaten earth, each subdivided by mud dams into small, floodable, pockets of cultivation. There are no straight lines to be seen anywhere as this is no vegetal parade ground, but rather a festival of assorted herbs, tomatoes, onions, sweetcorn, cucumber, aubergine, red kale, squashes and more. Decorative palm, olive, citrus, carob, pomegranate and pink pepper trees are welcome for their shade and produce, while the fabulous blue jacaranda and bright pink oleander offer a feast for the eyes.

The Boccara family are proud of their gardens. Charles is dismissive of his architectural work at Les Deux Tours, insisting that his aim was to build a paradise – 'that means trees and life, not buildings'. He is happiest when people compliment him on his wonderful garden which, of course, they invariably do.

LEFT These multi-coloured pumpkins have been harvested in June and the earth prepared for another crop.

BELOW The complexity of the community of trees which make the Jnane Tamsna such a rich ecological environment can be truly appreciated from this rooftop vantage point. The property beyond makes one last stand against aridity before the landscape turns ochre.

98 Gardens of Marrakesh

16. Jnane Tamsna

It takes the courage of your convictions to site a palm tree in the middle of an entrance doorway but courage and conviction are bywords for the Jnane Tamsna, an unusual guesthouse in the Palmery owned by ethnobotanist Gary Martin and his wife Meryanne Loum-Martin. The couple share a passion for Marrakesh and have combined their interests in architecture, anthropology, design and botany to make something new, based on the rich cultural history of the region. Meryanne has collected interior design accolades for her interpretation of Marrakesh style, while outside, Gary has done away with the conventional boundary between allotment and flower garden to create a decorative landscape larder based on the *arsat* model.

The Martins built the Jnane Tamsna in 2000 to express their personal vision of the good life: a place of integrity and tranquillity. Meryanne designed the buildings, using natural materials and local crafts people, with an emphasis on modern comfort and elegance. Respect for the spirit of the place comes first, but the couple also hold a strong belief that local culture benefits from a fresh perspective and are not afraid to add something new to the mix. This attitude extends to the garden which is Gary's domain. His design is informed by traditional garden types but is also contemporary in its concern for ecology and the meaning of gardens for future generations. Ethnobotany is the study of the interaction between people and plants and Gary is fascinated by the inextricable links between social and ecological worlds. His work on projects around the world has won him international prizes and he is director of the Global Diversity Foundation, which supports biodiversity in community projects on three continents. Given his profession it is not surprising that he wanted to make a garden which would reflect his belief that people and plants should flourish in harmony.

The clue to Gary's utopian vision is in the name Jnane. This is the plural of the word *janna*, traditionally a space planted with date palms and fruit trees, and including grape vines, which appears in the Koran as an explicit description of paradise. At the Jnane Tamsna, nature is encouraged to flow in and around the buildings in a seamless manner, free to live its life, like a favourite pet that is treated as a member of the family. There are changes of mood between different planted areas but these are felt like movements in a single orchestral work. Gary acknowledges that the great traditional garden types of the region are at the heart of his design. The overall structure has been inspired by the *arsat* model, with its mix of tall sheltering palms towering over a middle stratum of citrus, olive, pomegranate, fig and mulberry trees among others, with a lower level of seasonal vegetables. This has been overlaid with the kind of ornamental plants typical of a *bustan* garden, such as daturas, jasmine, pittosporum, roses, lavender, rosemary and other aromatic herbs. The term *bustan* is from the Persian *bu* meaning scented and *stan* meaning place. Originally this would have been a strictly ornamental garden centred on a water feature but Almohad historians used the word to mean an orchard with vegetables and flowers. Water has always featured, as both a life-giving necessity and a recreational pleasure, in these gardens, so Gary has embraced the awkward necessity of swimming pools in the spirit of a modern *agdal*, or ornamental pool. Lastly, the *riad* model of an enclosed, quadripartite garden, designed for respite and privacy has broadly influenced some areas. An explicit reference to the form is made in a conceptual 'riad without walls', where the cross-axial figure is lightly drawn in soil by fine *zellij*-lined water channels, and the four planting areas are dense with lush vegetation.

Gary has a healthy respect for tradition but he is not a purist trying to recreate gardens of the past, nor is he interested in confining himself to an 'authentic' plant palette. Not only would it be almost impossible to establish which plants fit the bill, it would, ironically, be against the very spirit of the past, in which new plants were constantly welcomed by horticulturalists keen to exploit their culinary, medicinal and commercial potential. The origin of a plant is not important, but it has to be suited to local conditions: aloes and agaves are a good choice. This is why, unlike most other establishments, there are no lawns at the Jnane Tamsna – they simply do not make sense. Grass requires a large amount of water, much of which evaporates under the hot sun, and is difficult to maintain in winter when temperatures fluctuate wildly.

The ecological profile of the garden is important in other ways too. Two areas have been designated as set-aside: one along a defunct irrigation channel which is subject to floods, and the other in an area of unproductive, chalky soil. These have produced spontaneous regeneration of many species which have disappeared from the arid, over-grazed land around, including wild asparagus, giant cane, medicinal herbs and beautiful wild flowers. Many of these species would have been valuable to local people in the very recent past but change has been precipitous, leading to an increasing disconnect between people in the city and their agricultural heritage. Gary has initiated a number of very successful 'edible schoolyard projects', such as that at the Ibn Abi Sofra primary school, based in a small part of the abandoned Agdal Bahmad of the Bahia Palace. In tending their own vegetable plots children learn where their food comes from, how to eat well and, hopefully, to love and respect the environment.

100 Gardens of Marrakesh

LEFT Courgette, chili, herbs, citrus and olives all bed down together in the sophisticated chaos of Gary's 'edible landscape' at Jnane Tamsna.

BELOW It is tempting to describe this garden as a post-modern, deconstructed exploration of the *riad* style, in which the form is liberated from its confining walls, allowing it to re-invent itself in the context of an open space such as that of the Jnane Tamsna. However, that may put some people off enjoying what is a very satisfying composition, using a minimum of expensive materials, to create a modern interpretation of the classic *riad* design.

RIGHT Horseshoe arches, smooth pearly floors and perfumed and exotic planting make for a delicious introduction to the main building at the Jnane Tamsna.

At the end of a busy day Gary and Meryanne stand observing the *Pandorea jasminoides* which embraces the rough bark of the entrance palm; and a robust, lengthy discussion ensues. What does the climber add to the composition, should it be trimmed, should it be transplanted – is it right? The discussion is not driven by pedantic attention to detail; it is more about content and context. Gary and Meryanne risked their very livelihood to garden in a meaningful manner, but their daring has paid off. Guests love being in a garden so full of surprise where fruit, vegetables and flowers live together in cosmopolitan profusion – a model for the paradise garden of the future?

102   Gardens of Marrakesh

17. The Beldi Country Club

LEFT A simple rail and post fence acts as the perfect perch for guinea fowl, showing themselves off against a backdrop of multi-coloured roses, bougainvillea covered pergolas, the smudgy purple of the High Atlas Mountains dusted with snow and a sweeping blue and white sky.

BELOW The Beldi is well-known for its spectacular display of roses which perfume the air in a way which has to be experienced to be believed.

The Beldi Country Club is a bucolic retreat for frazzled city dwellers, just a ten-minute drive from the Medina walls, in the direction of the Atlas Mountains. There is no golf course, no 'members only' rule or strictures to keep off the grass, just an ocean of gardens dotted with biscuit-coloured vernacular buildings. Owner Jean Dominique Leymarie explains that he wanted to create the feeling of a rural *douar* or village, with winding streets and gentle rammed earth architecture. Could this place be near in spirit to the garden city of Marrakesh described by travellers over the centuries? That may be a romantic notion but it is clear from the minute you arrive at the Beldi gates that romance is something Jean Dominique does well.

The perfume in the air is extraordinary. Before you catch even a glimpse of garden the delicate, complex scent of roses invades you like a magic potion conjured up by some benevolent jinn. The Rose Garden which welcomes visitors to the Beldi has understandably become the signature of the club. A wide, formal path flanked by

LEFT Jean Dominique believes the success of the garden is in large part due to the degree of autonomy he gives his gardeners to place plants in appropriate spots. The artisans responsible for the hard landscaping have also been given some design latitude, resulting in paths studded with a multitude of little decorative motifs.

BELOW All season long, brightly coloured roses will perfume the air of the nearby terrace, with its tall graceful arches constructed in terracotta briquette, known as *bejmat*.

RIGHT An artisan dressed in French '*bleu de travail*', passes straw through a handmade 'sieve' to break it up into suitably short lengths before mixing it with earth and lime to use as a building material.

104 Gardens of Marrakesh

tunnels of bougainvillea leads into the complex, but it is impossible not to stop and admire the sight of 13,330 rose bushes arranged in two blocks on either side of the central feature. This was the first garden created on the site in 2005. Marrakesh had a thriving rose production industry, based at La Targa, which collapsed after Independence in the 1950s, but Jean Dominique was keen not to use commercial varieties. He sourced his more rustic stock from old gardeners who had worked in the industry as young men and who still had knowledge of what they call country roses. It is perhaps this piecemeal approach to gathering his plants which has produced the charming rural meadow effect, with roses of all hues seemingly placed randomly, without any self-conscious attempt at artful colour-coordinated drifts. Roses feature widely in the city, indeed Marrakesh is often referred to as 'the rose among the palms' and they have been used en masse in municipal bedding schemes such as those near the airport. The difference here is that, while relating to contemporary ideas of simplicity and clean volumes, they also connect with an Islamic respect for nature which believes that plants should be allowed to express their true personality.

The Arabic word *beldi* translates as traditional, but in Morocco it evokes the authenticity of country life, of things well made in an artisanal fashion, and a certain pride in native culture. Beldi is also a variety of olive much grown in the region which is cured at different stages of maturity to produce fruit of every shade from green to pink, purple and black. The two meanings come together on this site with the olive trees of the original plot integrated into the garden and the clear commitment to traditional construction materials and artisanal decoration. The traditional and the olive are both present in the intimate, neutral toned, courtyard garden which follows the Rose Garden. The space is enclosed by walls constructed in *pisé* using local clay mixed with straw. The straw is visible in the finished surface, chopped up but fresh looking, as if the walls were made of dung from a farmyard. A collection of old, country-style wooden doors, decorated with geometric designs, is displayed against the walls, with a single olive tree standing tall in the centre of the space – *beldi*.

Jean Dominique modestly declares that he is no garden expert but, as in all the best gardens, it is his personality and vision which has shaped the guiding principles here. He resists the notion of design, saying that the gardens developed gradually as land became available, one following the other, each expressing a different idea but looped together loosely in a promenade. He favours a spontaneous approach to garden making: a basic idea, followed by the gathering of plant material (often at his favourite garden centre, Casa Botanica, owned by plant expert Sadek Tazi),

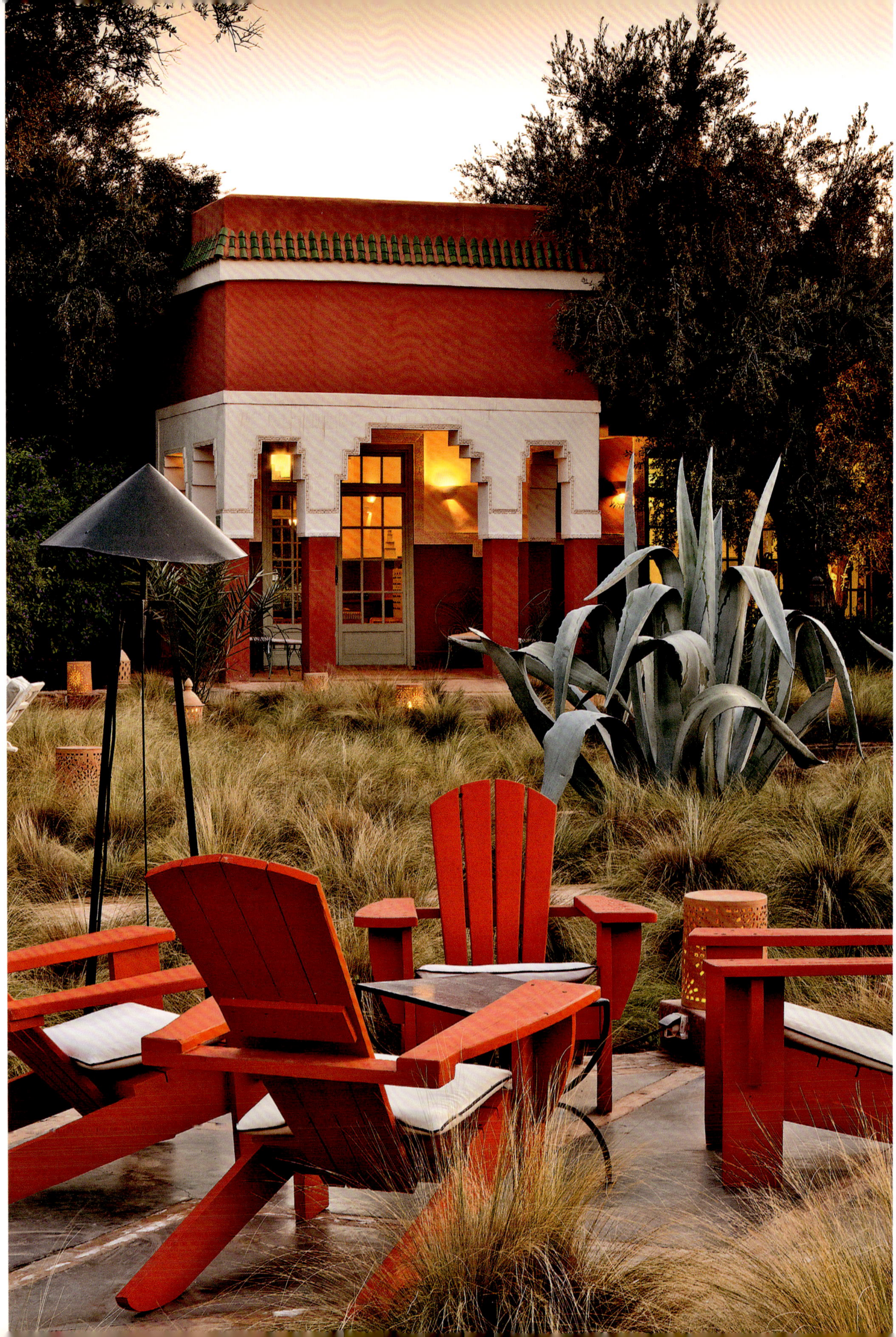

which is then planted up in collaboration with his team of gardeners. He admits that he sometimes has to tweak the results but believes that involving the gardeners at this level gives them a particular pride and sense of achievement which bears fruit. The artisans responsible for the hard landscaping have been given the same liberty, creating charming pebble motifs in the paths.

This relaxed approach has its risks and Leymarie shakes his head in frustration when he points out that the Riad Garden has not worked. The intention was to create a traditional *riad* design, quadripartite, with a central fountain and orange trees. The problem here is that it is too rustic. The success of a *riad* garden depends on the use of fine materials, a strict geometry and a range of traditional plants. The inclusion of benches made from twisted branches and country-style materials confuses the design. However, elsewhere the technique has paid dividends. The Grass Garden contains a series of 'hideouts' where guests can sit privately with a drink among the shimmering stems of fountain grass, set with large specimen agaves. While the design is thoroughly modern there is an informal, playful quality here which shakes off any 'designer look'. The Pampas Pool has two rows of stately pampas grass (*Cortaderia selloana*) lining a rill flowing into a small square pool. It is hard to believe that this is the much maligned seventies favourite as their white plumes shine in the late October sun, alive with small birds feeding on the seed heads. There is much to enjoy elsewhere: the humorous dichotomy of the Agave Pool where a shallow square pool is studded in the four corners and central island with drought-resistant *Agave americana*; the Small Cactus Garden; the tiny corridors of the Botanic Garden or the 'walls' made from large terracotta pots stacked on simple wooden shelves in the Lily Pool Garden.

As evening closes in, the birdsong becomes clamorous and conversation halts for a moment to enjoy the recital. This is a happy, healthy garden, one which Jean Dominique describes as Eden as he mounts his battered cream bicycle to go and check on his mischievous flock of guinea fowl.

LEFT In the Grass Garden angular Adirondack-style chairs, painted a punchy tomato soup red, are a match for muscular agave.

RIGHT ABOVE *Cortaderia selloana* (Pampas Grass) is an unusual choice for the margins of this water rill.

RIGHT CENTRE Boulders have been spread over an extensive area and decorated with groups of variegated *Agave marginata* and *Agave americana,* in a dry garden with the obvious benefit of being low maintenance.

RIGHT BELOW Locally made terracotta pots have been imaginatively transformed into an interesting feature wall.

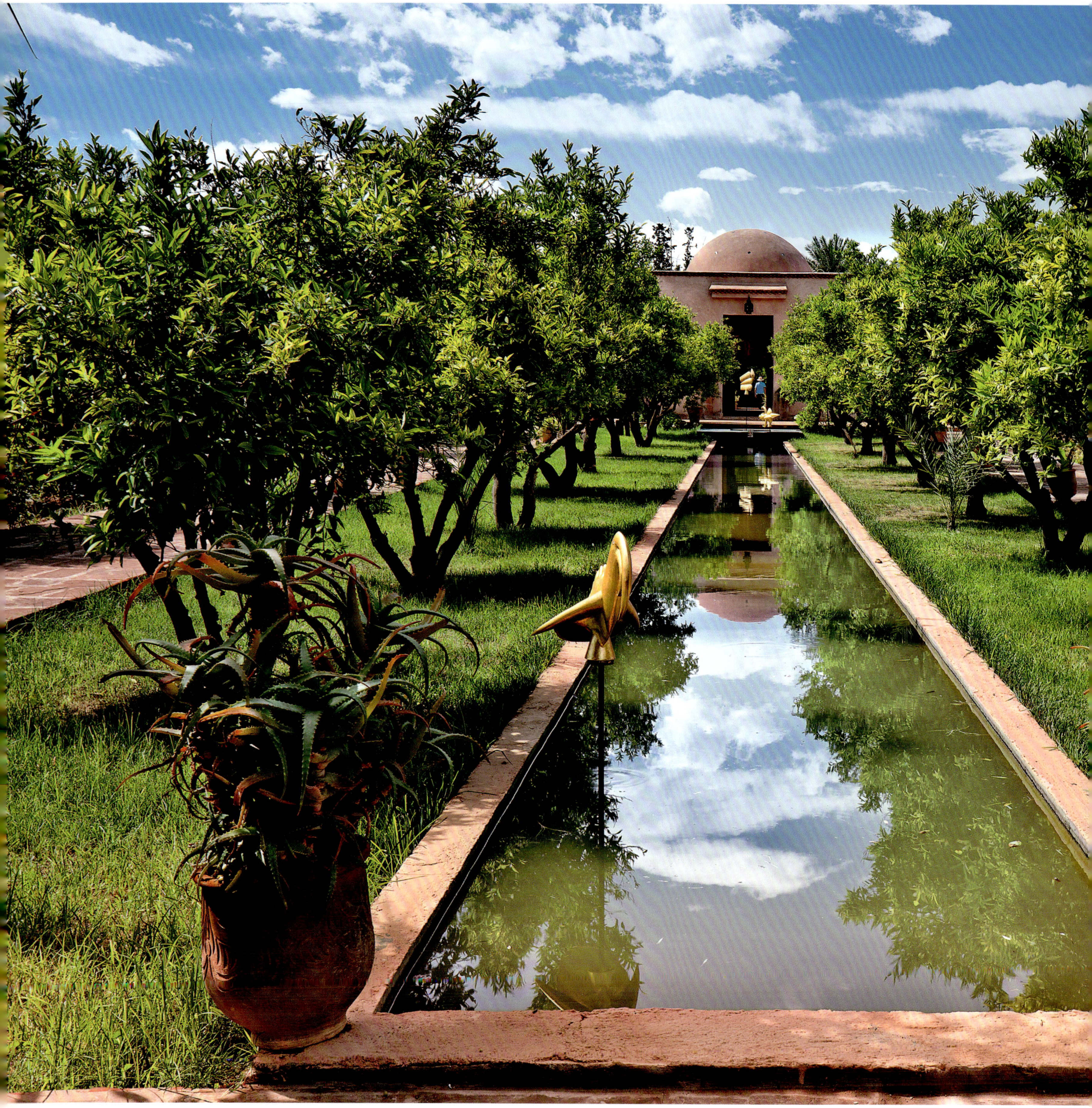

18. Gardens of the Musée de la Palmeraie

LEFT A long, narrow canal, centred on a former stable block crowned with a beautiful *bejmat* cupola, is the dominant motif of a garden inspired by Moorish Andalusia. Orange trees, set in flanking grass strips, add rhythm with pots of unruly *Aloe vera* for piquancy. Gold birds by sculptor Claire Thiam look like sophisticated city dwellers enjoying a pastoral moment.

Abderrazzak Benchaabane is a tall, stylish and imposing man in his fifties who gives the impression that he does not suffer fools gladly. However, in conversation he is both generous and poetic, confessing to two grand passions in life: contemporary Moroccan art and nature. As an ethnobotanist he holds strong views on the power of gardens to touch a chord in the human spirit. Reflecting on why we garden, he believes that the desire to enchant others and communicate the wonder of nature is at the heart of the urge to make gardens. Art has a similar role, only coming alive when it has a public. In 1999 he acquired a plot of orchards among which he built his home. But it was the cluster of beautiful farm buildings on the site which inspired the idea of a museum in which his considerable collection of contemporary Moroccan art, and gardens, would be cultural bedfellows. Ten years in the making, the Musée de la Palmeraie (Palmery Museum) opened to the public in May 2011.

There are three distinct gardens to discover beyond the beautiful whitewashed exhibition hall, crowned by its cupola made from small flat bricks known as *bejmat*. The first of these, the Andalusian Garden, is orientated on an axis with the main building and features a long central canal flanked with rows of Seville orange trees (*Citrus aurantium*) set in strips of lawn. A stand of mature date palms acts as a backstop, their fringed fronds creating a fan shape behind the rhythmic pompom forms of the oranges. It is loosely inspired by the Moorish gardens of Southern Spain, and in particular that of the Generalife in Granada. However, the idea is kept simple with materials such as stone flags and terracotta tiles in tune with the rural feel. The water in the canal is still and, unashamedly, full of algae, producing the pleasing effect of vivid green velvet, the perfect foil for the golden bird sculptures which add a touch of glamour. Terracotta pots of different shapes are carefully placed to give a visual rhythm to the flow of the design. They are planted as if they were individual vases containing a bouquet, each one different, with no intent to match or echo each other. Flowering plants are incidents within the garden, their colour a device to lure the viewer to take a closer look.

This subtle approach to planting is evident in the Water Garden but here the same elements are used to different effect. The Water Garden lies beyond the Andalusian Garden and is dominated by a large, natural-shaped pool edged with smooth, rounded boulders like giant pebbles. They have a nostalgic significance for Benchaabane, reminding him of hours spent as a child by country streams, but more importantly, he explains, 'a boulder in a stream becomes an island around which a community of life can organise itself'. Toads and tortoises use them as sunbeds here, and small birds as a bar from which to take a drink. The atmosphere in this garden is of bucolic calm with a pretty kiosk, topped by traditional green glazed tiles, inviting a moment of relaxed reflection. If the Andalusian garden is a metaphor for the historic past and political conquest, the Water Garden is about the countryside and the desert way of life in which the oasis is a hub of felicity.

In contrast the third and final garden exploits the emotional dissonance experienced in a display of tough prickly survivors which elicits feelings of both wonder and discomfort. There is nothing pretty, or gentle, or reassuring about the Cactus Garden. It is a space which challenges our notions of what a garden should be and what it is for, so in this sense it reflects some of the debate around modern art. Indeed the garden is contained in a rectangle of old *pisé* walls whose thickness and height act very much as a frame around a painting. There is just one breach in these walls, through which the garden is entered at ninety degrees to the axial design. The whole garden is boldly planted with groups of cactus and succulents, with two paths dividing the space longitudinally into three areas. At the far end is a studio for an artist in residence.

There is something shocking yet fascinating about being surrounded by these plants, perhaps the horticultural equivalent to keeping snakes as pets. The scene is harsh and stark, in contrast to the cactus garden of the Majorelle with its fountains and brightly-coloured hard landscaping. This garden celebrates these ancient inhabitants of a semi-arid landscape and respects their particular beauty without compromise.

Benchaabane's love of cactus began in early life through watching American Westerns. A visit to Latin America and a chance meeting with Hans Thiemann confirmed his interest in these plants whose resistance to a hostile environment impressed him. Thiemann, a German horticultural engineer, founded his cactus nursery on the outskirts of Marrakesh in 1963. Today it is one of the largest cactus plantations in the world producing over one hundred and fifty varieties, mainly from Latin America. Although very secretive about his knowledge, Thiemann eventually advised that cactus should not be treated like other garden plants as they were 'wild' and had their own rhythms which needed to be respected. Their shallow roots can easily be damaged by over watering so it is best

LEFT The water garden at the Musée de la Palmeraie is based on Benchaabane's childhood memory of running free in a rural village with boulder-edged streams and pools filled with wildlife.

ABOVE Another great joy of his youth was watching Hollywood Westerns which sowed the seed of his passion for cacti. In this walled world, cacti of all shapes and sizes rule supreme with each individual a personality in its own right.

to let them manage summer drought in their own way. By following his advice Benchaabane has created the ultimate low maintenance, eco-garden which is remarkably free from disease.

While the three gardens at the Palmery Museum are not strictly speaking conceptual gardens they have been created in something of the same spirit. They are designed to make us see gardens as more than just a collection of plants put together to pleasing effect and they demand that we think of them as meaningful works of art with cultural and emotional content. But, above all, Benchaabane advises one guiding principle, *'il faut étonner les autres'*, you have to surprise people – something he does with aplomb.

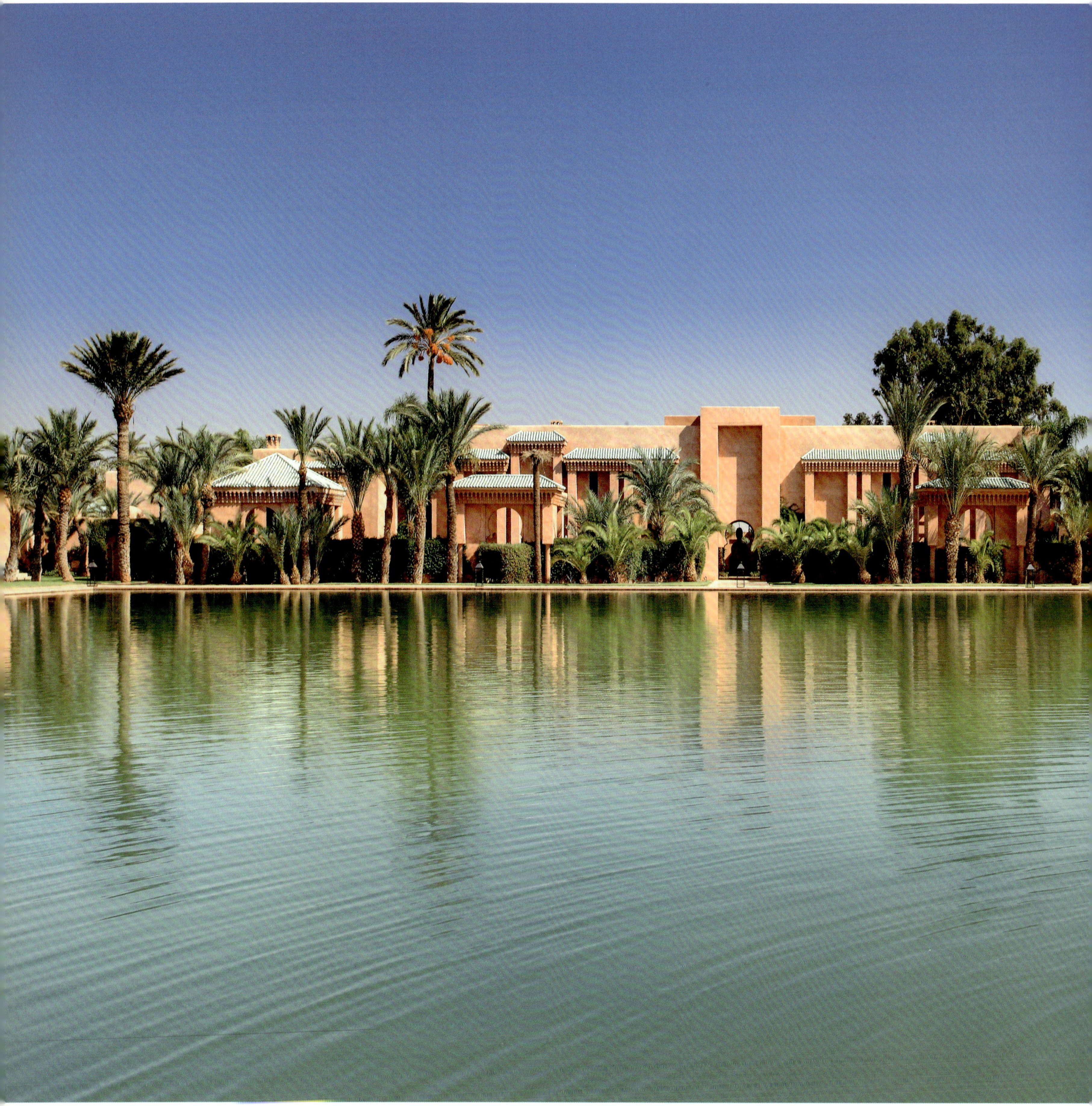

19. Amanjena

LEFT The silken surface of the *sahrij* at Amanjena is disturbed, setting off a kinetic show of ripples under a peerless sky, watched by various members of the palm family.

Amanjena is a luxury boutique hotel belonging to the Aman Resorts group, situated in the Palmery. Everything here is immaculate with the kind of effortless, cool chic of Grace Kelly. Even the staff look the part. Dressed in beautifully designed uniforms, they seem to glide rather than walk, greeting every visitor with the customary gesture of hand on heart and the refrain, '*salaam aleikum*' (peace be upon you). Peace is embedded in the hotel's name: *aman* is Urdu for peace, and *jena* is a version of the Arabic *jannah* which translates as heaven or beautiful garden. The challenge for architect Ed Tuttle was to do justice to the name Amanjena and create a 'peaceful paradise' within easy reach of the tumultuous city.

Tuttle, an American born in Seattle in 1945, has designed several of the legendary Aman hotels, including the first one in Phuket which opened in 1987. He has created a house style in which minimalist architecture is conceived to complement the natural and cultural setting of the project. Passionate about design, Tuttle controls the look of everything, from the building itself to the interior decoration and gardens. This approach led him to immerse himself in the life of the city in order to distil the essence of Marrakesh as the basis for his interpretation. His goal was to create a space which reconciled three opposing perspectives: past with future, luxury with necessity, artisan with high tech. The resulting Amanjena is a fascinating essay on his response to the city, which has been described variously as 'Zen meets Arab-Andalusia', 'airbrushed ethnicity' and 'Bauhaus Star Wars'.

The six hectare site, bought in 1998, lies on the Route de Ouarzazate in the Palmery and consisted of olive groves and wheat fields, peppered with tall palms and the occasional venerable tree. It is encompassed by the Amelkis Golf Club, with the celebrated Royal Golf across the road. The journey from here to the Medina takes just fifteen minutes and much of the route is lined with wide ribbons of public gardens with clipped orange trees, exotic shrubs and fountains. This was the context for Tuttle's design in which he took two principal ideas from his exploration of Marrakshi culture: privacy and discretion and the life-giving force of water in the oasis. The entrance to Amanjena is so discreet that it is easy to miss, with the apricot-coloured façade presenting a blank face, except for the huge horseshoe arched doorway. There are no conventional hotel rooms, guests have their own unit, varying in size, but always with a spacious private patio garden. 'It's a very interior architecture,' Tuttle explains,' from the road you don't know what it is. As you enter it reveals itself bit by bit.' This last is not entirely the case as the view from the entrance pavilion, with its soaring vaulted ceiling, leads the eye directly onto the shimmering heart of the site, a magnificent, deep-green water basin or *sahrij*.

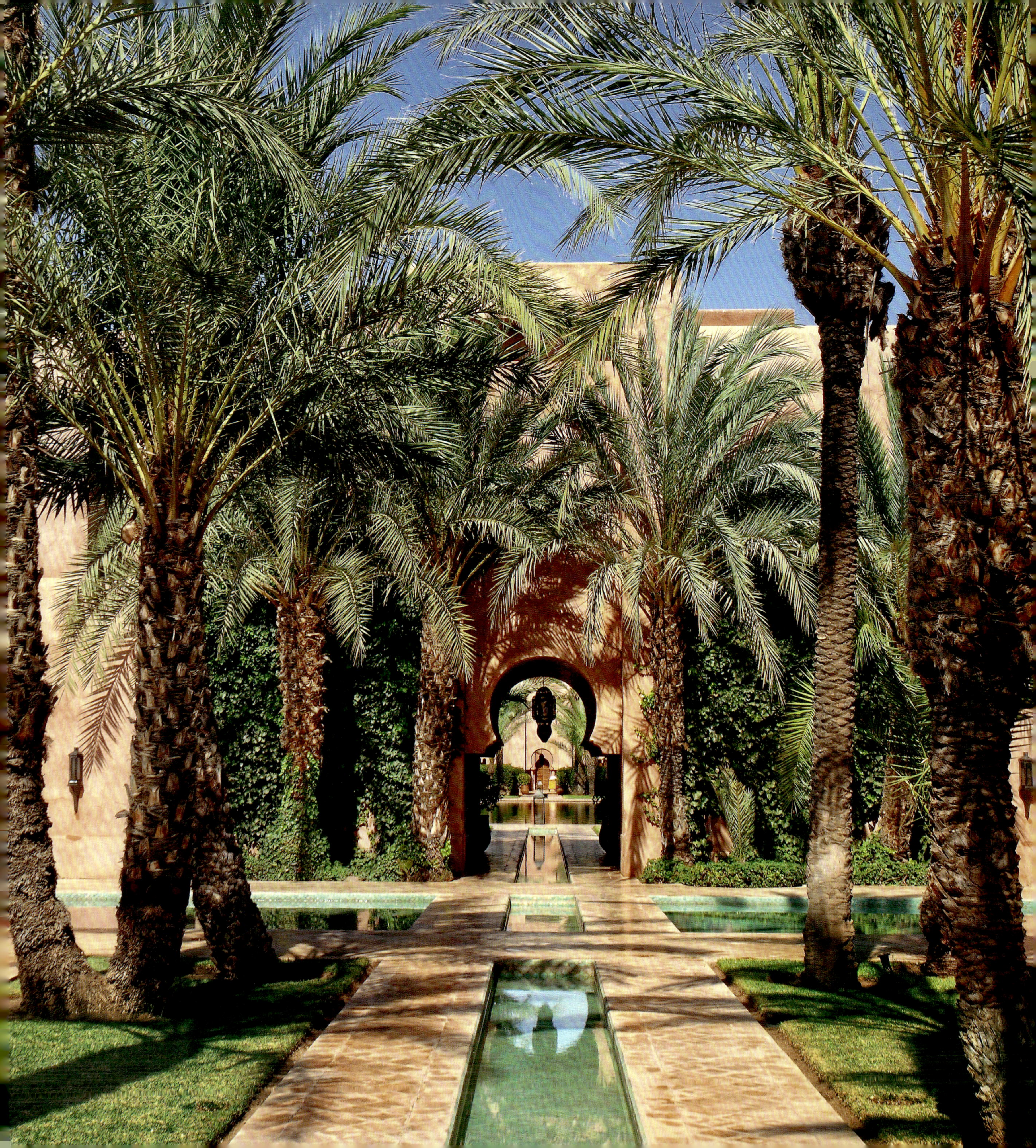

LEFT At Amanjena the *sahrij* is flanked on either side by canal gardens embellished by palms. It requires a great deal of hard, physical work to keep these looking trim as they need to have the fibrous sheath, left by old fronds, removed to reveal the trunk beneath.

BELOW Pale turquoise, fish-scale tiles give this canal an understated elegance. The view would have ended in the golf course beyond but a cleverly sited pavilion turns the design back in on itself.

The site already possessed a small irrigation tank, reputedly dating from the Almoravid period, which served the farm. Tuttle recognised the emotional value of this feature, with its links to the past, especially to the iconic imperial basins of the Menara and Agdal. Their grid-based layout, with wide walkways between blocks of planting, also provided the blueprint for his design. However, while the design of the imperial basins reaches out with long sight lines into the surrounding landscape, Tuttle turned this aesthetic in on itself, with architecture on all four sides of his central water feature, rather like a spare version of the Badi Palace. The original basin was enlarged giving it a gentle and pleasingly balanced rectangular shape 60m x 65m; big enough to be impressive but small enough not to be threatening. The sight of this block of water as one walks out of the lobby is both surprising and arresting. The composition is entirely successful, with the proportions of the architecture and the rhythm created by palm trees creating a theatrical set piece to wonder at. The whole is given an extra dimension as the feature acts as a giant mirror, doubling up the exotic planting in an inverted image on the water whose movement imitates the blur of a mirage. As a resident Great Blue Heron elegantly swoops down to fish it seems that even the wildlife has been specially selected. Tuttle's basin is a geometric oasis with every element orchestrated to Albertian perfection. It is a fine example of how an ancient motif can be pushed to the limits to create a modern masterpiece.

It is a difficult act to follow but Tuttle uses water again to great effect in the two parallel canal gardens which flank the *sahrij* on the other side of the basin suites. These shallow canals owe much to Moorish Andalusia and to the design of the Badi Palace with its central basin and flanking pools. They are tiled with thousands of hand-cut, pale turquoise *zellij* in a fish-scale design, which sparkle in the strong sunshine. Several varieties of palm have been used to give height and variety to the skyline as they stand guard over the precious water. The tallest of them are date palms which have been preserved from the original site. In fact Tuttle has taken pains to accommodate as many venerable trees as possible into the design, even where they interfere with his preference for strict geometry. Some have become the focal point of the private gardens which, in contrast to the public areas, are intimate and relaxed. Of course they contain every material comfort but they are intended to be 'a little taste of paradise', with walls clad in scented climbers, citrus of

BELOW Trimmed dwarf pomegranate (*Punica granatum* 'Nana') has been used to make this Zen Garden, which relies on the white crushed-stone being constantly raked into perfect order to best show it off. Not an easy task in this well used area.

BELOW Amanjena was developed on the site of an old olive grove and some of these trees have been incorporated into the garden design as seen here.

every description perfuming the air, or offering their warm fruit, and 'bouquets' of potted flowering plants. Many of the old olive trees have also been saved, either in the private gardens or in informal spaces such as the grassed barbeque area which has a wonderful view of the Atlas Mountains. The olives are harvested and pressed for oil which supplies the kitchen throughout the year.

Amanjena opened in 2000, so the gardens, which are intimately linked to its architecture, have had time to mature and balance the buildings. The restrained colour palette and spare ornamentation used throughout may not epitomise the colourful Marrakesh of the souks but Tuttle defends this choice saying, 'I wanted the hotel to look nomadic'. His vision of a heavenly garden, in the context of a city which has been greatly influenced by the desert way of life, is that of the oasis. As night falls and lanterns are lit, his basin shimmers with the reflection of palm fronds and in the still of the evening it is easy to feel the power of Amanjena, a peaceful paradise.

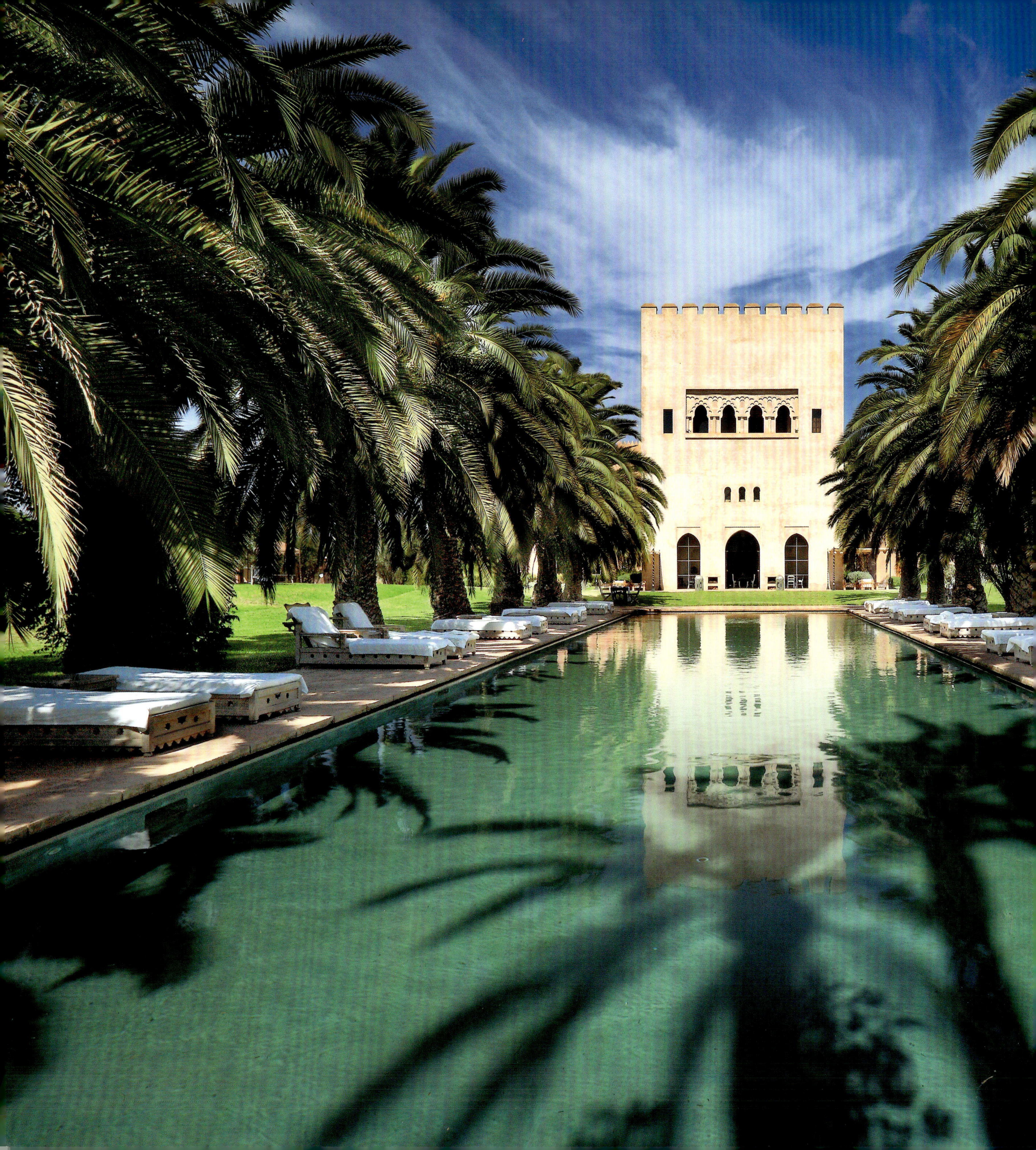

20. Ksar Char-Bagh

LEFT All actors have their 'best side' and some gardens do too. This view at the Ksar Char-Bagh gets people excited but would be nothing without the magnificent rows of fifty-year-old Canary Island Palms (*Phoenix canariensis*) which have been lovingly cared for since their installation nearly a decade ago.

BELOW There is a definitely medieval, heraldic theme in parts of the garden, including a pet falcon in the olive tree.

Nicole Grandsire LeVillair has that seemingly effortless, pared down chic which must be due to a genetic modification in Parisian women. The same could be said of the gardens she has created over a ten year period at the Ksar Char-Bagh. Situated in the Palmery, the 3.5 hectare site is divided up into a series of themed gardens which reveal Nicole's familiarity with garden history, her sensitivity towards local tradition and, perhaps more than anything, her desire to engage thoughtfully with the meaning of garden making.

Nicole and her husband Patrick came to Marrakesh to change their lives: to exchange cool Parisian skies for sunlight and warmth, and their predictable professional routine for a new challenge. In just two years they created a luxury, country house hotel, the Ksar Char-Bagh, whose name sums up their design principles: *ksar* is Berber for a fort or fortified village and *char-bagh* is derived from the Persian for four (*char*) and garden (*bagh*), which has come to be identified with Islamic quadripartite gardens incorporating the four rivers of paradise described in the Koran. Both elements have been interpreted loosely by the couple, with the finished building being more palatial than its Berber namesake and the gardens expressing the life-giving force of water without the geometric form of a *char-bagh*. The result is imposing, fortress-like architecture, rising from a skirt of garden landscapes embroidered with watercourses and pools.

The entrance to the garden is guarded by a large bird of prey chained in an olive tree. He is a surprisingly heraldic emblem but his presence begins to make sense as the path turns smartly at a right angle to present the façade of the main building. This is certainly local architecture but the similarity to a medieval French *chateau-fort* is striking. Rectangular pools of shallow water lap at the walls, and

LEFT ABOVE Undulating blocks of *Drosanthemum speciosum* form carpets of green clouds for eleven months of the year at Ksar Char-Bagh but in spring they are transformed into a mass of pink petals.

LEFT BELOW The heart of the house belongs to Andalusia in a fine courtyard modelled on the Court of Myrtles in the Alhambra.

RIGHT The Jardin Anglais represents for Nicole the English love of informal, natural-looking gardens.

120 Gardens of Marrakesh

a path traversing large blocks of planting is like a drawbridge. Nicole has cleverly used a rampant succulent (*Drosanthemum speciosum*) as ground cover, painting the area with what she describes as a 'carpet of green clouds' but which could equally represent an algae-filled moat. The design is both modern and timeless, a quality which Nicole admires. She lists her favourite designers as Vita Sackville-West, Russell Page, Christopher Bradley-Hole, Louis Benech, Jean Mus and Mien Ruys, and in a way the work of these major figures reflects this dichotomy. Keen not to copy slavishly the ideas of these greats, Nicole has understood their individual design vocabularies and uses phrases here and there to tell her own garden story.

There is a strong medieval theme throughout the garden. The design makes two points: that the simple, geometric forms of these gardens are in tune with modern ideas; and that the emotional content of humanised nature can only be fully appreciated in the context of the wild. At the heart of the Ksar Char-Bagh is a courtyard whose design pays homage to the great medieval Moorish gardens of Spain, and particularly to the Courtyard of the Myrtles in the Alhambra Palace. The proportions of the rectangular canal with its flanking strips of planting are successfully reproduced, but Nicole has replaced the myrtle hedges with a repeating pattern of her own design. Contrasting green and grey shrubs have been trimmed to suggest a chevron figure with spots on a backcloth of green velvet grass. Green and grey was a favourite combination of Russell Page in his stylish parterre gardens. Here the design is reminiscent of bold heraldic motifs, softened by the inclusion of orange trees.

The swimming pool to the rear of the property echoes the proportions of the central Alhambra courtyard in a consciously repeated pattern. Nicole has planted rows of beautiful *Phoenix canariensis* along its length to complete the conceit. Beyond the pool is the decorative vegetable garden inspired by medieval French potagers, with planting areas defined by low wooden hurdles and hedges of rosemary and box. This highly controlled space gives way to an eerily beautiful, 'untouched' area, where a piece of natural Palmery landscape, pale and dry, with a few humble adobe buildings like a ghostly hamlet, is a reminder of the age-old struggle between man and nature. The *Jardin à l'anglaise* expresses another aspect of that relationship – the Romantic idea that nature knows best and in which natural plant forms are celebrated. Nicole has interpreted this approach in a free-form garden consisting of groups of shrubs of varying height and habit, where each plant has been left free to express its true nature.

Agricultural landscapes form a buffer zone between highly controlled gardens and natural scenery. Nicole completes her story with a nod to agricultural practices in the region. Irrigation techniques are crucial to successful farming in this semi-arid land. Traditional open channels known as *seguias* carry water to where it is needed. At the Ksar Char-Bagh they have been elevated to become decorative as well as practical elements. Some are lined with a mosaic of pebbles, rising from sculptural mounds or briefly ducking underground in swirling basins. Others have been treated more strictly, made to flow in crisp-edged, straight lines, which zigzag through areas of planting. There is a natural pond for wildfowl, surrounded by a grove of bamboo which is harvested for use on the property. A deep stone basin, sheltered from the sun by a canopy of bamboo, is stocked with fish. Finally, there is the olive grove, planted with already mature specimens in large blocks; they have a poetry of their own with their graceful forms and shimmering grey leaves. This has been reinforced by interspersed blocks of fountain grass whose feathery heads add touches of gold sparkle to the silver notes of the olive trees.

The circle is complete and we are back to the beginning in a car park lined with old London black cabs used to ferry visitors around. The spell is broken and it is time to leave. The hawk looks down imperiously from its heraldic perch as if brief entry to this world has only been granted by his munificence.

LEFT Part of the garden is modelled on the working landscape of the Palmery with its date palms and old system of irrigation channels. At the Ksar Char-Bagh these channels have been lined with a mosaic of small pebbles which, elsewhere, are used to emphasise other water features such as springs and little bubbling fountains.

RIGHT ABOVE The fish pool is deep and cool with antecedents in a patrician past.

RIGHT BELOW The graphic quality of the olive grove has been complemented by cartouches of feathery *Pennisetum setaceum* which add a little poetry. Originally these were intended to be planted with corn but it did not do well and of course was more work in that it had to be sown annually.

Visiting the Gardens

The gardens featured fall into two categories: those which are open to the public (with or without an entrance fee) and guest house and hotel gardens which require you to use their bar or restaurant or, as in the case of the Riad Madani, are only accessible if you choose to stay there. Generally people in Marrakesh are very generous and pleased to help when they can – if you speak French it is a plus. It is possible to hire an officially licensed, English speaking, Moroccan guide who will be able to enrich your overall experience of the city – your hotel should be able to help. Where charged at all, entrance fees to public sites are modest, so it is appreciated if you have small change to hand.

All information was correct at the time of going to press but it is always worth checking opening times ahead of a visit. Be aware that because Arabic script has been transliterated, there are often several ways of spelling the names of people and places but they should sound approximately the same when said aloud. Some sites have no formal address and no contact details.

1 The Agdal
South of the Grand Méchouar in the south of the city. It is a long walk from the centre of town (4km) so it is advisable to take a taxi and ask it to wait to take you back – a visit will not take long.
No contact details available.
Open Fridays and Sundays, 08.00–17.30. Closed when the king is in residence. Free entry.

2 The Menara
South-west of the city, at the end of the Avenue de la Menara, about 2km from the Koutoubia Mosque.
No contact details available.
Open daily, 08.00–18.00. Free entry but a small charge to visit the poolside pavilion, which closes for lunch 12.30–15.00.

3 Gardens of the Koutoubia
The Koutoubia Mosque is on the Avenue Mohammed V, with the Park Princess Lalla Hasna (Koutoubia Gardens) on the Avenue Houman el Fetouaki.
No contact details available.
Open daily, sunrise to sunset. Free entry.

4 The Badi Palace
Pass through the gate at the south end of the Place Ferblantiers, turn right and walk to the end of the blind alley flanked by high walls in front of you.
No contact details available.
Open daily, 08.30–11.45 and 14.30–17.45. Modest charge.

5 The Bahia Palace
Rue Riad Zitoun el Jedid, in the south-east of the city, near the Mellah quarter.
No contact details available. Open daily, 08.45–11.45 and 14.45–17.45, except Friday, when lunchtime closing is extended from 11.30–15.00. Modest charge.
NOTE: The Marble Courtyard and the Grand Riad are closed to the public during an extensive renovation programme due to be completed by the end of 2013.

6 Dar Si Said
Derb el Bahia. On leaving the Bahia Palace turn right, back up the Rue Riad Zitoun el Jdid and right again, through an archway which faces a small car park. Turn first left at a water fountain and the museum is a short walk away.
No contact details.
Open daily, except Tuesdays, 09.00–12.15 and 15.00–18.15. Modest charge.

7 Riad Mounia
Riad Zitoun Kedim, Derb Jdid No 66, Medina, Marrakesh.
Tel: 00 212 (0)5 2442 7690, www.riad-mounia.com

8 Riad Enija
Rahba Lakdima, Derb Mesfioui No 9, Medina, Marrakesh.
Tel: 00 212 (0)5 2444 0926, www.riadenija.com
The Enija welcomes non-residents for lunch and dinner, including a visit of the gardens. Phone in advance to make a reservation.

9 Riad Madani
64 Derb Moulay Abdelkadar, off Derb Dabachi, Medina, Marrakesh.
Tel: 00 212 (0)5 2444 1884, www.riadmadani.com
This is a private home which welcomes guests in a country house atmosphere. Unfortunately the only way to experience the riad is by booking in as a resident.

10 The Mamounia Hotel
Avenue Bab Jdid, 40040, Medina, Marrakesh.
Tel: 00 212 (0)5 24 388 600, www.mamounia.com
The hotel usually welcomes well dressed, non-residents for drinks, lunch or dinner, unless they are very busy. Walk straight through to the terrace at the rear for drinks overlooking the gardens.

11 Arsat Moulay Abdeslam Cyber Park
Avenue Mohammed V, Medina, Marrakesh.
www.arsatmoulayabdeslam.ma
Open daily, 09.00–19.00. Free entry.

12 Jnane el Harti
Rue Cadi Ayad, off Place du 16 Novembre, Gueliz, Marrakesh.
No contact details available.
Open daily, 08.30–17.30. Free entry.

13 Jardin Majorelle
Rue Yves Saint Laurent, 40090, Marrakesh.
Tel: 00 212 (0)5 24 313 047, www.jardinmajorelle.com
Open daily. 1 October–30 April: 08.00–17.30, 1 May–30 September: 08.00–18.00. During Ramadan (which changes dates each year): 09.00–17.00. Entrance charge.
The Café Bousafsaf in the gardens serves very nice snacks and meals throughout opening times: 00 212 (0)5 24 303 779 to make a reservation.

14 The Palais Rhoul
Dar Tounsi km 5, Route de Fes, 44000 Marrakesh.
Tel: 00 212 (0)5 24 329 494, www.palaisrhoul.com
All-inclusive spa days are available to non-residents including use of the gardens. Telephone for more details and to make a reservation.

15 Les Deux Tours
Douar Abiad, Circuit de la Palmeraie, BP 513, 40000, Marrakesh.
Tel: 00 212 (0)5 24 329 527, www.les-deuxtours.com
Les Deux Tours welcomes non-residents to their restaurant and spa. Always telephone in advance to make a reservation.

16 Jnane Tamsna
Douar Abiad, La Palmeraie, Marrakesh.
Tel: 00 212 (0)5 24 328 484, www.jnanetamsna.com
Jnane Tamsna offers a wide range of interesting activities for all the family. Gardeners will enjoy their guided tours of the Palmery with its unique oasis ecology. For details contact sarahjnane@gmail.com. Non-residents are invited to book for a swim, organic lunch and a leisurely stroll around the gardens.

17 The Beldi Country Club
Km 6, Route du Barrage, 'Cherifia', Marrakesh.
Tel: 00 212 (0)5 24 383 950, www.beldicountryclub.com
The Beldi is open to all who wish to reserve a place by the pool, spa treatments and/or lunch. For details and map see website.

18 Musée de la Palmeraie
Dar Tounsi, Route de Fes, opposite Metro, Marrakesh.
Tel: 00 212 610 408 096, www.museepalmeraie.com
Open daily, 09.00–18.00. Entrance charge.

19 Amanjena
Route de Ouarzazate km12, Marrakesh.
Tel: 00 212 (0)5 24 399 000, www.amanresorts.com/amanjena
The hotel restaurants and bar are open to non-residents. Telephone to make a reservation.

20 Ksar Char-Bagh
Djnan Abiaf, Palmeraie, BP 2449, 40000 Marrakesh.
Tel: 00 212 (0)524 329 244, www.ksarcharbagh.com
Anyone is welcome to book for lunch or dinner and it is also possible to spend a day relaxing by the pool after a massage or hamman. On Saturdays a special Berber lunch is served in the rustic setting of the old farm buildings and brunch by the pool is a Sunday treat.

Glossary

Adobe sun-dried brick made of clay and straw.
Agdal vast productive orchard and pleasure garden with irrigation basin.
Arsat, **arset** or **arsa** large, irrigated, productive plot in an urban context often doubling as a pleasure garden.
Bayha joy, felicity.
Bayoud disease affecting date palms caused by the fungus *Fusarium oxysporum*.
Bejmat natural-coloured terracotta tiles originally from Fes, rectangular or square in shape.
Beldi Arabic term for traditional, authentic. A variety of olive.
Borj fortified Berber tower.
Buhayra literally 'little sea', the Arabic term for the Berber word 'agdal'.
Bustan Persian for a scented flower garden but in Marrakesh has long been used as a more general term meaning orchards with interplanted vegetables and flowers.
Calèche horse-drawn carriage.
Char-bagh or **chahar bagh** quadripartite garden design deriving from Persian for four and garden.
Dahir decree.
Daliya vine trained on trellis placed overhead to provide shade.
Dar large house with more than one storey.
Derb lane.
Douar rural hamlet or village.
Jnane, **jnan** or **jannah** garden planted with palms, fruit trees and vines and, in the Koran, referring specifically to paradise.
Khettara ancient hydraulic system of bringing water to the city by means of underground channels which tap into an aquifer. 'Qanat' in Persian.
Khossa cup-shaped fountain.
Koutoubeen traders in books and manuscripts.
Ksar Berber for fortress or fortified village.
Leuh rammed earth construction.
Maalem master craftsman.
Medersa or **madrasa** school for Islamic studies.
Medina old walled city.
Menzeh pavilion.
Patio the interior courtyard of a dar, completely paved and without planted areas.
Pisé rammed earth.
Quermoud green enamelled roof tiles used on buildings of standing such as mosques, palaces and the homes of the gentry.
Riad planted urban courtyard, usually rectangular in shape and entirely enclosed by walls or buildings.
Sahrij large irrigation basin.
Seguia irrigation channel.
Tadelakt a type of stucco, polished with black soap to give a smooth, luminous finish, typical of Marrakesh.
Zellij enamelled terracotta tiles.

Select Bibliography

Achva Benzinberg Stein, *Morocco Courtyards and Gardens*, The Monacelli Press, USA, 2007.

Emma Clark, *The Art of the Islamic Garden*, The Crowood Press, United Kingdom, 2004.

Mohammed El Faïz, Rachid Benaoud, *Jardins de Marrakech*, Actes Sud, France, 2000.

Mohammed El Faïz, *Marrakech: Patrimoine en Péril*, Actes Sud, France, 2002.

D. Fairchild Ruggles, *Islamic Gardens and Landscapes*, University of Pennsylvania Press, USA, 2008.

Jean Gallotti, *Le Jardin et la Maison Arabes au Maroc*, Actes Sud, France, 2008 (first edition 1926).

Narjess Ghachem-Benkirane, Philippe Saharoff, *Marrakech Demeures et Jardins Secrets*, ACR Edition, France, 1990.

Penelope Hobhouse, *Plants in Garden History*, Pavilion Books, United Kingdom, 1992.

Massimo Listri, Daniel Rey, *Marrakech: Living on the Edge of the Desert*, IdeArte, Italy 2005.

Gavin Maxwell, *Lords of the Atlas: Adventure, Mystery, and Intrigue in Morocco, 1893–1956*, The Lyons Press, USA, 2000 (first edition 1966).

Edith Wharton, *In Morocco*, Tauris Parke Paperbacks, USA, 2008 (first edition 1920).

Quentin Wilbaux, Michel Lebrun, *Marrakesh: The Secret of Courtyard Houses*, ACR Edition, France, 1999.

Acknowledgments

Writing this book has been an adventure in which I have been accompanied by many generous and spirited people who have opened my eyes to what it means to garden here. I owe a debt of gratitude to them all, especially to the garden owners who have put their trust in me. My special thanks to El habi Ait Ali, Abderrazzak Benchaabane, Aziz Cherkaoui, Colin Kilkenny and Maryvonne Grunberg for setting me on the right track. A big thank you also to Alessio Mei for his unfailing energy, consummate professionalism and sense of humour and to his partner, Charlotte Royle, for help with plant names. Obviously the support of my husband Desmond and children Thomas, Sophia and Joshua has been very important and is always a source of joy. My greatest thanks are reserved for my mother, Gloria Mudaliar Hutchinson, whose love of gardening and Marrakesh has been an inspiration.

Index

A
Abd el Moumen, Sultan 15, 21, 27, 28
Abdeslam, Moulay 69
agdal 15, 21, 37, 41, 99, 126
Agdal, The 4, 7, 14–19, 21, 23, 27, 31, 32, 37, 41, 115, 124
Ahmed ben Moussa (Bahmad) 37, 41, 43, 45, 99
Ahmed el Mansour, Sultan 31, 32, 34, 35
Alaouite dynasty 37
Al-haj Yaish 16
Alhambra Palace 32, 120, 121
Ali ben Youssef, Sultan 7
Almohad dynasty 7, 15, 21, 28, 31, 37, 99
Almoravid dynasty 7, 15, 28, 115
Amanjena 112–17, 125
Andalusia 18, 21, 29, 31, 35, 47, 109, 110, 113, 116, 120
Arsat Moulay Abdeslam Cyber Park 7, 66, 68–73, 124
arsat, arset, arsa 7, 10, 46, 47, 63, 65, 66, 67, 69, 71, 72, 99, 126
Atlas Mountains (*see also* High Atlas Mountains) 15, 16, 21, 23, 35, 41, 43, 103, 117
Avenue de la Menara 21
Avenue Mohammed V 10, 69, 75

B
Bab Berrima 31
Bab el-Mahzan 21
Bab Khemis 53
Badi Palace, The 7, 30–35, 37, 115, 124
Bahia Palace, The 7, 36–41, 43, 47, 71, 99, 124
Bahmad (*see* Ahmed ben Moussa)
bayha 10, 126
Bayoud 13, 126

Beaucé, Thierry de 58
Beldi Country Club, The 102–107, 125
Belkziz, Souad 78
Ben Aicha 24
Benchaabane, Abderrazzak 87, 109, 110, 111
Berber 10, 15, 57, 71, 76, 77, 87, 119
Bergé, Pierre 86, 87
Boccara, Charles 93
Boccara, Mathieu 97
borj 15, 126
Bouachrine, Grand Vizier 47
buhayra 15, 18, 126
bustan 99, 126

C
Casa Botanica 105
Conerdings, Björn 51, 54
Cox, Madison 87
Crystal Pavilion, The (Badi Palace) 32

D
dahir 10, 126
daliya 10, 57, 126
dar 7, 43, 47, 51, 126
Dar el Hujar 28
Dar Si Said 7, 42–45, 47, 124
Djebilet 21
douar 10, 93, 103, 126

E
El Achak, Karim 71
el Faïz, Mohammed 10, 37
el-Mesfioui, Haj Mohammed ben el-Mekki 37

F
Fes 47, 51
Foundation Mohammed VI for the Protection of the Environment 71
French Protectorate 7, 10, 71, 81

G
Gallotti, Jean 47
Garcia, Jacques 63, 65, 66
Gardens of the Koutoubia 26–29, 124
Gardens of the Musée de la Palmeraie 108–111, 125
Generalife, The 109
Gibraltar 18
Global Diversity Foundation 99
Grandsire LeVillair, Nicole 119, 120, 121, 122
Grandsire LeVillair, Patrick 119
Grunberg, Alain 47
Grunberg, Maryvonne 47, 49

H
Haldimann, Ursula 51, 53, 54
High Atlas Mountains 4, 7, 57, 77, 103
Hollywood 13, 89, 91, 93, 111

I
Ibn Abi Sofra 99
International Association of Francophone Mayors 76
Islam 7, 10, 21, 23, 27, 35, 43, 47, 51, 54, 63, 75, 81, 93, 105, 119
Issil, river 10

J
Jardin Bouachrine 46, 47
Jardin Majorelle 80–87, 95, 110, 125
Jnane el Harti 74–79, 125
Jnane Tamsna 13, 98–101, 125

K
khettara 16, 126
khossa 42, 47, 126
Koran 37, 43, 75, 99, 119
Koutoubia Gardens (Park Princess Lalla Hasna) 26, 29

Koutoubia Mosque 4, 7, 10, 23, 24, 26, 27, 28, 29
Ksar Char-Bagh 118–23, 125

L
Lamghari, Aziz 91
Les Deux Tours 13, 92–97, 125
Leymarie, Jean Dominique 103, 104, 105, 107
Louis XIV 18, 24
Loum-Martin, Meryanne 99, 101

M
Machry, Homero 57, 58, 59
Madani el Glaoui, Grand Vizier 57
Majorelle Blue 60, 83, 85, 86, 87
Majorelle, Jacques 10, 81, 86
Mamoun, Moulay 63, 67, 71
Mamounia Gardens, The 62–67, 124
Mamounia Hotel 7, 71, 124
Marble Courtyard, The (Bahia Palace) 37, 41
Marchisio, Antoine 63
Marie-Anne, Princess of Conti 23
Martin, Gary 13, 99, 101
Mazet, Jean Charles 71
Mecca 27
Medina, The 7, 10, 13, 15, 21, 27, 29, 31, 34, 41, 47, 51, 57, 65, 66, 69, 75, 103, 113, 126
Meknes 24, 35
Mellah, The 31
Menara, The 7, 15, 20–25, 27, 37, 115, 124
menzeh (pavilion) 23, 66, 75, 126
Mohammed ben Abdallah, Sultan 63, 69
Mohammed IV, Sultan 16
Mohammed VI, King of Morocco 7
Montaigne, Michel de 32
Moroccan Ministry of Cultural Affairs 37

Moulay Abd al-Aziz, Sultan 43
Moulay Ismail, Sultan 23, 24
Musée de la Palmeraie, Gardens of the 108–111, 125
Museum of Moroccan Arts 43

N
New Town, The 7, 10, 75

O
oasis 10, 15, 19, 29, 91, 93, 95, 110, 113, 115, 117
Orwell, George 75

P
Palais Rhoul, The 13, 88–91, 125
Palmery, The 7, 10, 13, 89, 93, 99, 113, 119, 122, 123
paradise 7, 15, 43, 75, 97, 99, 101, 113–116, 117
Park Princess Lalla Hasna 29
patio (*ouest ed-dar*) 7, 42, 43, 51, 53, 126
Pavilion of the Fifty (Badi Palace) 32
Petit Riad (Bahia Palace) 37, 39
Pisa 32
pisé 7, 19, 105, 110, 126
Place Ferblantiers 30
Place Jemaa el-Fna 7, 69, 71
potager 67, 93, 95, 122
Prost, Léon-Henri 63, 75, 77

Q
quermoud 43, 126

R
rammed earth 7, 15, 34, 77, 93, 103
riad 7, 27, 31, 32, 37, 41, 43, 45, 47, 49, 51, 53, 54, 57, 58, 99, 101, 107, 126
Riad Enija 43, 50–55, 124
Riad Madani 43, 56–61, 124
Riad Mounia 43, 46–49, 124
Riad Si Moussa or Grand Riad (Bahia Palace) 37, 41

S
Saadian dynasty 31
sahrij 26, 47, 113, 115, 116, 126
Sahrij el Gharsyya 18
Sahrij el Hana (Tank of Health) 16, 18
Saint Laurent, Yves 86, 87
School of Moroccan Architecture 37
seqqaya (wall fountain) 42, 49, 60
Si Said ben Moussa 43, 45
Sidi Mohammed, Sultan 22, 23, 47
Sidi Moussa 41
Sinon, Paul 81
souks 7, 10, 51, 57, 117

T
T'hami el Glaoui, 57
Tazi, Sadek 105
Thiam, Claire 109
Thiemann, Hans 110
Three Kings, Battle of the 31
Tuttle, Ed 113, 115, 116, 117

U
urban farm 10, 41

V
Versailles 15, 18
Villa Oasis 81, 87

Y
Yacoub el Mansour, Sultan 31

Z
zellij 31, 32, 35, 37, 42, 43, 47, 51, 63, 99, 116, 126
zitoun 46, 47
Zohra, Lalla 28